A Road of Rescued Hearts

Stories of trust, miracles, and the lessons horses teach us.

For permission requests, contact the author directly via email at: Elowynhaleauthor@gmail.com

First Edition

ISBN: 979-8-9927932-0-8

Printed in the United States of America

Edited by Justin Rajkowski

Cover Design by Elowyn Hale

I0459320

Dedicated to my mother Catherine. Thank you for a lifetime of instilling hope, love, and horses in my soul. We have been through the dark and made it to the light.

This book is further dedicated to the individuals and organizations committed to the noble mission of rescuing and rehabilitating these magnificent creatures.

And to the horses like those who built me; the patient, the recovering, and those who crawl out of their own dark pasts to look at a new human and give them a chance to help, this book is for you. Bless your gentle souls.

Disclaimer

This book, while based on true events, is for entertainment purposes only and is not intended as a reference guide for equine training, or nutrition. These stories may include some now outdated and now unpopular training methods, personal risk decisions, and activities which the author is not encouraging readers to take on themselves.

Rescuing horses, while both possible and rewarding, often presents significant dangers. Animals that have experienced abuse or negligent care require experienced handlers and owners who can attend to their complex physical and mental needs along with a professional team of caregivers.

Furthermore, it is important to acknowledge that within every industry mentioned in this book, there are exemplary owners. While bad ownership leads to problems, good ownership fosters healthy, thriving horses. Some names, locations, and scenarios have been altered to protect privacy.

I Have to go Feed the Horses

I must make the statement "I have to go feed the horses" a million times a year.

I say it sometimes with love, sometimes with general disinterest and even sometimes I admit, with annoyance.

I say it over grain and square bales and round bales and supplements, mash and medication tubes and horse pills.

I say it morning noon and night sun rain wind snow sleet hail or heck.... tornado a couple times if I am being honest.

It is a beautifully simple statement that means so much more.

When have I said this other than the harsh weather days?

Other than the days I was so tired I wanted to go back to bed?

Other than the nights after a long full day, when my feet ache and my back aches and my mind aches for a break?

I say it when things are dark. I say it when things

have me so down, I cannot think of any other reason to get off the couch and out of my own dark clouds.

I say it when the world is cruel. When I lose someone or something I love and have no other reason to move forward.

I say it when I get home from a trip and realize just how lucky I am for my amazing creatures who embody my heart walking around outside my body.

I say it when I'm happy, gloomy, or devastated.

Such a simple sentence and process with so much stability.

It calls us to a task greater than ourselves. To love and care for others.

In return, each time I utter these words my feet magically deliver me to my greatest gifts, my safe space, my 1000lb therapists. And they are always ready to greet me.

So next time your horse friend says "I have to go feed the horses" recognize that within that small statement lies a profound guiding force in their days.

Chores rarely have only physical benefits.

Introduction

I was only six when I entered the horse world. A typical Midwest kid of the 90's complete with strawberry blonde pigtails, a windbreaker track suit in neon colors, and an embarrassing amount of unibrow. I went through the stereotypical "I want a pony" phase a year earlier at age five. For most kids, that phase fades away eventually when sports, friends, or the allure of teenage independence come calling. For me, however, that yearning only deepened. Every Breyer model horse, every new halter, every bale of hay pushed the level higher, and each passing year added more fuel to a fire. Even now, I've never been able to extinguish it.

Our big Victorian house in the country saw its fair share of rehabs, and its fair share of strange equine escapades. As a child, it was a magical place to grow up where the whole property was fenced, and so the horses roamed where they liked, even directly next to the house. I was fortunate enough to grow up with my herd right at the front porch and sleeping outside the bay window as I napped on the couch just inside. My mother was fortunate enough - we say with a wink - to get to plant new flowers constantly after our lovely lawn ornaments ate and slept on the flowerbeds. We used to joke about the horses laying out in what should have been her manicured areas of the property being our beautiful flowers. Life on that small farm was a whirlwind of animals, fresh air, and countless adventures. I learned early on that being around livestock wasn't just about feeding, grooming, and riding. It was about responsibility, patience, and resilience. Night checks sometimes involved trudging through ankle-deep mud or navigating snowstorms to check on the horse in the barn, my legs, in their muddy muck boots weighed down by exhaustion and my heart racing with worry until I saw each pair of glowing eyes reflecting in the beam of our flashlights through the door cracks. We weathered many storms together, both literal and figurative; through sickness, injuries, and the gut wrenching goodbyes that are all parts of horse ownership.

There were horses that came and went - some because it was time, and others when it felt like it was far too soon. Those losses are the hardest, and even years later, they still leave an ache that is hard to describe. I had dreams and the start of a promising show career, with all the ribbons and accolades a young rider could envision; and was well on my way to that golden future at one time. That path, however, took an unexpected turn when family circumstances changed. Divorce left the home, life, and dreams I had as a child and teen in tatters. But through it all, the horses remained my constant. Even when the show circuits became out of reach, my love for these animals never waned. My mother and I continued to care for them the best we could, despite our darkest days seeing us losing our home, our family structure, and our security. As for the horses in this book, not all were highly trained or pedigreed show horses. In fact, most were not. But as many know, the mutts, the mixes, the mysteries have just as profound an impact without 'impressive' papers. Every one of them made a mark whether through their quiet companionship or their wild, untamed spirit on some incredibly damaged parts of my life.

Throughout this book, you'll meet a colorful cast of characters - horses who have shaped me in ways I never imagined. Their stories span years of growth, heartbreak, and learning. You'll encounter tales of triumph and defeat, sorrow, and joy. It's important to understand that these stories are not told chronologically, so you may encounter stories where I had not yet learned lessons I learned in other stories.

In addition, it is vital to understand that not every horse was under our ownership, and my role in their lives was sometimes limited by circumstances beyond my control. There were moments when decisions had to be made based on what was available at the time, without the benefits of today's technology or medical advances. I know so much more now these many years into my journey and am thankful for a never-ending growth and education mindset that led me to my current state of knowledge. My choices in these stories were guided by love, but they were sometimes constrained by the situation at hand. I did what I could, when I could, always striving to do what was right.

It's been an incredible journey thus far; one filled with more twists and turns sometimes than expected - perhaps we should label those parts as a 'heck of a ride' instead. And yet, I find myself eager for whatever comes next, with a heart that remains tethered to these incredible animals.

Lastly, for my non-horsey readers: thank you for venturing into a world that might seem foreign or intimidating at first glance. I hope this book serves as a gentle guide through the highs and lows of horse life, and I've included a glossary of terms in the back to make your experience smoother.

Welcome to the ride - I promise, it's one worth taking.

{Chapter 1}

Broken by the Track - Bottle Rocket

I was only six years old. Leaning on the top rail at the racetrack with the wind in my face, light up tennis shoes balanced on the second rail and bouncing with glee. The small group of adults and I watched the shining bay horses trot around the sandy racetrack at a working pace. Even at partial race pace they seemed to fly, to tell even the wind to make haste or get out of the way as they went whooshing past us mere humans leaning on the railing. Training season was in full swing, and the Standardbred farm was buzzing with activity. The energy in the air was tangible as I watched my parents assess one horse in particular as the group made their way around.

He was not as impressive as the other horses as he hauled the yellow and black sulky cart behind him at the brisk trot. Most of the others were towering over sixteen hands, beautiful and powerful muscles in every stride. The little bay drawing my parents' attention though was at minimum six inches shorter at the shoulder; perhaps barely touching fourteen-two hands. He was a two-year-old and my parents had been asked to 'go in on' with a group of investors from work. Their first venture into owning a racehorse. Following my request the previous spring for my first pony, it was a way for them to possibly make some money and get me through the 'pony phase' nearly every little girl will go through at one stage or another.

My mother had never mentioned horses to me when I was little, even though the love for them ran deep in her heart too. A bad situation years past had resulted in a suitor stealing and selling her horses Major and Catastrophe for spite when she turned down a marriage proposal – now that's the way to get the girl- and she had sworn in her heartbreak over her two lost companions that she would never own horses again. That plan was working out for her until the day I sat on the bottom stairs of our old Victorian home and cried. The most important request my six-year old heart had ever realized it needed to make. I was terrified to be turned down.

Even at just six, I remember a fear growing in my heart; the fear that I might never have a horse. I couldn't put it into words, but I knew with absolute certainty that they were what my heart needed to be happy, and that no doll, no toy, and no amount of candy or cuddly puppies could fill that void. Being around horses was what my heart yearned for, what my soul seemed to crave.

I remember first voicing my request to my parents. It wasn't a casual, off-the-cuff request for a pony like you'd expect from a little girl infatuated by a Barbie horse in the store or who wanted to ride the pony ride at the fair. Sitting on the bottom step in our Victorian parlor near the bay window I began to cry.

Mostly with the anticipation of being told no. When they checked on me, I asked with such sincerity that my mother told me they were a bit taken aback. I remember their exchanged cautious, uncertain glances parents often do, and after a moment, they

answered with a hesitant, "Maybe." I clung to that "maybe" like a lifeline, even though I could sense their reservations. Looking back, I can understand why they hesitated.

Apparently, the signs had been there all along. Long before I could articulate what I wanted I'd reach out for every horse we passed by. It didn't matter if they were trotting proudly down the main street in a parade, or if they were standing still behind a fence as part of some historical attraction or tour. I'd stretch my tiny arms towards them and lean out of my parents' arms with a fierce determination that would turn into fits and tears if we didn't get close enough for my liking. Yet, the second I was granted access to these towering, intimidating creatures, I'd often burst into tears again out of fear. The sheer size and power of these "big, scary monsters," was overwhelming. As a note - I did the same thing with the Easter Bunny once, but I didn't want to go near him with those giant chompers in the first place!

I imagine it was more than a little confusing for them—my eagerness and fear waging war with one another in the most dramatic of ways. To them, I must have seemed like an emotional whirlwind. They must have wondered if my passion would hold steady, or if I'd lose interest once confronted by the reality of what I was asking for.

But even through all that crying and confusion, the pull never lessened. It was like some invisible force kept drawing me back, whispering that horses were where I truly belonged. The tears of fear weren't because I didn't want to be near them, they were because I didn't yet understand how to be near them. It was a yearning for connection that I was too young to comprehend, and yet it was too strong to ignore. So, I waited on a maybe, knowing it may never come to pass. But here we were the next spring watching this little shining dark chocolate colored stallion pace around the track. Even though he was tiny the trainer assured us they expected him to maintain pace with the others and that he on a regular basis, proving to be faster. He had 'it' - whatever that was. I didn't know what 'it' was at that age, but my parents seemed pleased. So, they agreed with one minor change to the agreement. Everyone else in the group would have to find a different horse, because my mother was buying this one outright. Although not the easiest way, she stated that if he ever got hurt, ever was ruined for the track, she wouldn't have others' opinions on if he was put down or not just because it was the convenient or cheap way out. And so, although he still resided at the track, we purchased Bottle Rocket – aka Rocky – the fastest tiny horse in the Midwest.

We soon found that Rocky was not so loving. A clever stallion that could Houdini his way out of the stall every day. Each morning would attempt to attack whoever came in first and found him standing in the main aisle waiting for them. Initially another lock was added to the stall. A different kind, this one was harder to open, and the problem was forgotten; until it happened again, and again. Another lock, another incident, another lock, and on and on it went. Until at last a lock was placed on the bottom of the stall door that latched into a drilled hole in the concrete floor. No horse that small could undo all these and reach that bottom lock. Right?

After Houdini-ing his way out of the floor lock, the announcement was made to my parents that the trainer would not and could not train this horse as a stallion anymore. He had become too smart and too dangerous to handle. The decision to geld him was made and after healing up, Bottle Rocket was put back into training preparing for his first big debut race – sans attitude. While his times were as good as ever, his speed continuously impressive, tragedy has a way of finding the most promising things and asserting its dominance over hope.

Two days prior to the race during some final

practice laps. Dark clouds gathered as a storm was blowing in. The session was going to be cut short. The other Sulkys were starting to pull in one after another. Last lap! Then he would be back in his stall safe and dry. It began to pour, and puddles formed. No issue, the cart would go through small amounts of mud and water. Half a track was left, a quarter, an eighth. Then it happened. A bolt of lightning hit the track not far in front of the pair and Rocket broke from his full stretch striding pace buckling his back leg in the process.

The vets were called, the trainer was consulted, and my parents were contacted about the news. The outlook wasn't good. Rocky would certainly never race. In fact, he may never heal. The best choice they said would be to put him down. Thank goodness for my mother's foresight on the issue, the others all said put him down, the trainer said put him down. The vets said it could be cheaper in the long run to get a different horse and try again. So naturally, the never ridden, now ex-racehorse was brought to the local boarding facility to be trained into my first "pony" instead. While at the facility, while healing, he was given strict accommodation plans. Including not to be put into the pen with the farms "crowning glory" a large and quite nasty stallion named Banner. Banner towered over Rocky at over sixteen-two hands tall; and had a habit of beating up other horses for sport. I remember the day my mother and I went early to visit Rocky and found him cowering in the corner of Banners pen. He had bumps and cuts all over him and that facility immediately had one less patron. Rocky came home to our small acreage and his own new fence, with a newly repurposed antique carriage house for

a barn. The healing process was long, and Rocky took several years off to heal, and then following his restarting as a riding horse we learned together. Being a cart horse, he hadn't been ridden much, even with the trainer we later found out. Though I had participated in lessons on broke school ponies, I was still a beginner rider, now around 8 years old in my slick seat oversized black western saddle when the time finally came for Rocky and I to work together. He is to this day the bumpiest horse I have ridden and had a bad habit of bolting here and there on the trainer's lunge line with me aboard but looking back I have to say he tried his best considering the situation. I grew up loving him and quite a few others joined along the way. Rocket never went lame again on his bad leg, and in fact went to trail class at the county fair with some girls who were older than me in the riding program my mother had enrolled me in. He did wonderfully. A couple summers later I taught him to work in an English saddle for walk trot classes. Anyone who has worked with a riding standardbred knows that they are not the most comfortable ride, so posting in an English saddle helps!

Associating it with the accident, Rocket was afraid of water for years. Not afraid of rain, or a bath, but of puddles in particular. One day at the fair I watched in great amusement as my mother forgot this fact, walking ahead of the horse and through a long puddle which ran across the width of the path they were on. She quickly got to the end of the rope and found out that Rocky was no longer with her. In fact, he was leaning at an angle which seemed downright impossible over the puddle. He had gone as far as he could, toes touching the water and was looking like he would topple forward if he leaned or stretched his neck out even one centimeter more. He made a lot of people laugh that day, but it was a sad reality which lurked behind the horse everyone thought was funny. His incident haunted him, as did anything yellow and black (a hot wire fence, a truck that went by one day) because that was the color of the sulky cart he pulled on that horrible day.

Now my mother and I had worked with Rocky to get him past puddles. We would flood the large garden area when it was not planted just to get him to walk through the deep dark mud and splash. He would work his way through it after an hour or so and the next day we started over again. It never improved a great deal or stayed consistent. So naturally when we made the seven-mile roadside trail ride to our favorite nearby creek I knew he simply wouldn't go in and play with the other horses. He approached the water and snorted, looking around in a panic. I had my boy on a forty-foot lunge line and stood in the water so he would hopefully come to me in trust, but he stood fast, leaning comically as he once had over a puddle years earlier at the fair. The sand bar where he stood was incredibly soft. As he leaned and teetered over the shallow water, I watched as the sand gave way, sagging and relinquishing its structure sending him in a hollow plop into the water.

I will never forget the plethora of expressions which crossed that horse's face when he went into the water. He stood clumsily staggering to his feet and looked to me as if I had done it! How dare you? He seemed to say.

Then I watched as he decided he had bigger things to worry about, he was IN the water, up to his knees surely it would try to grab him, it would hurt him, something terrible would happen. And I must give it to my mare Luna, who you will read about later in this book. She really helped me out! Luna was a playful mare who loved water and would spend long minutes just lazing around in it up to her back if she could find a spot deep enough. She didn't let Rock figure things out for long; she did the nongraceful horse version of a belly flop laying down to roll, sending a small wave his way and absolutely soaked him. She then proceeded to roll over, legs kicking through the water and soaking me as well as finishing off any hope Rock had of remaining dry.

I guess he must have considered his day an adventure at that point because he began to walk through the creek. He trembled, and snorted, looking a bit like I imagine a barefoot person would if they didn't know where the loaded mouse trap was in the dark. One step, two, three, at this point he launched into the most joyous bucking fit I have ever seen, crow hopping and leaping for the sky, before pawing the water and rolling, and rolling, and rolling. He was the 'water horse' before we left for home that day, and he really showed Luna how it was done.

The end to Rocks story is a mystery to me. I imagine by now he would be playing in the puddles in the sky. I like to think when it rains, that's the splashes from his joyous splendor. The ending to Rocks story was ripped from me when my family came on hard times. Hard times, the darkest times really; seldom leave one with options they like. Because of some key players in my mother's and I's life, making choices we all had to live with, we were forced to rehome Rocket, My first horse, My friend. He was auctioned through a charity organization, and we hear he went west to Oklahoma with his new owner. While we have been assured that the new owner loved him, this story will always be a hole in my heart. I raged quietly inside for years following the situations which made it necessary to abandon my horse. The sense of powerlessness was all encompassing.

As an adult I have spent years scouring the sale sites, the kill pen listings, the social media ads and searching his name again and again in hopes he may just pop up on a search. We aren't meant to know the ending to all the tales it would seem, but I hope if I get to any version of heaven eternal that my search for him will be over when he meets me at the gate (odds are he will have figured out the latch) and I cannot wait to go make a splash together.

{Chapter 2}

Learning to Love the Rescue – Lucky

Lucky's story is a short one, though that doesn't make it any less significant. It's mostly brief because I was quite young when my mother and her close friend took him in, and many of the details are blurred by the haze of childhood memory. I don't remember the exact day Lucky came into our lives, but I remember the feeling; an electric mix of excitement and sadness, when I overheard the adults talking about him. A little bay pony had been picked up by a friend of a friend. He was coming from an abusive situation and was in desperate need of a safe place to land. Unfortunately, his rescuer didn't have the resources to keep him for long, so my mother and her friend, who had become somewhat of a local refuge for horses in need, decided to step in.

Lucky was a plain little gelding of unknown breed and background, with no distinctive markings to set him apart. An unremarkable bay, he was a dull shade of brown, as if even his coat had given up trying to shine. His hair was coarse and lifeless, his hooves were long and cracked, and his eyes were perpetually draining, evidence of untreated health issues. What I remember most vividly though was the fear radiating off him like a physical force. He would flinch at the mere sight of people and tremble when anyone tried to approach.

The day he arrived at my mother's friend's property is lost to me, as are the first days of his stay. But I do remember the shift that began to happen after the adults spent day after day trying to earn his trust. They took turns standing quietly outside or just inside his pen, offering food and kind words, hoping to convince him that not all people were monsters.

Slowly, very slowly, they managed to get close enough to see another health concern they had suspected from the start: his legs were covered in botfly eggs. For those unfamiliar, botflies are parasitic insects that lay their eggs on warm-blooded hosts like horses. These tiny, sticky eggs attach to the horse's hairs, waiting for the slightest lick or brush of a muzzle to transfer them to the animal's mouth. From there, depending on the type of botfly, the larvae either burrow into the skin or travel down into the digestive tract, where they grow and feed, causing discomfort and potential health complications. In Lucky's case, his neglected state meant he likely had been carrying these parasites, as well as others I am sure for quite some time.

We needed to do something about his time sensitive conditions before they caused more damage, but there was one glaring problem: no one could get close enough to touch him yet. Handling Lucky wasn't just a matter of cleaning his legs, or trimming his feet, or treating his eyes - it was a matter of rebuilding his shattered trust. The adults debated

the best course of action until finally, someone suggested that maybe, just maybe, I could be the answer. Being small and less threatening, the adults thought I might succeed where their best intentions had failed.

That's how I found myself standing in the round pen, holding a small grooming block and a bucket of baked apple biscuits. I was far from unfamiliar with being around horses. We had owned Rocky, my first horse, for a couple of years. But I was careful to follow the instructions I was given all the same. It was with the happiest of hearts that I got to participate. Kids love to have a job, and I loved helping more than anything. Not to mention it feels downright cool as a kid when you can do something the adults couldn't. I knew to speak in the soft, reassuring voice I used with our other horse and not to make quick movements. Knew where the kick range was, and how to watch the horses' ears. I also had three adults on standby if it appeared that Lucky would reject my approach in any dangerous way.

At first, Lucky stood rooted to the spot along the fence rail, his eyes wide and nostrils flaring as he watched me with suspicion. I remember holding my breath, barely daring to move for fear of scaring him as I extended my hand, offering one of the biscuits and averted my eyes. Horses are prey animals, and humans are predators. Our eyes and their orientation on the front of our heads flag us as inherently dangerous to a horse that has not been taught otherwise. That day minutes stretched into what felt like hours and my arm became tired before he finally took a tentative step forward, then another. When his muzzle brushed my palm to snatch the biscuit, I nearly cried out in joy, but I stayed quiet, knowing that even the slightest startle could send him back into the shadows of his fear.

He retreated immediately to the outskirts of the pen to chew his treat in solitude. But he had trusted, and that was the best first step.

Every day after that, I'd return to the pen, armed with a pocketful of treats and a whole bucket of hope. Bit by bit, Lucky began to trust, and within a few days, I was able to scrape the bot eggs from his legs while he stood as still as a statue with his head in a bucket of grain. The fear in his eyes began to be replaced with a wary acceptance and I'd chat with him as I worked. I couldn't begin to tell you what we chatted about now that I am older, but I'm sure I was telling him all the little things a child thinks are important, what I had for lunch, which of my classmates had the coolest toys, and how brave I thought he was. I know I started telling him he was beautiful, even if his body wasn't. My mother had taught me well, it's what's on the inside that counts and all that glitters is not gold. It's funny how much I felt he understood, even back then. Our connection grew, not through force or fear, but through shared moments of vulnerability and quiet.

Now, you might be wondering: Why would any parent let a young child handle a scared, flighty horse in a round pen alone? The answer is simple is, my mom could read horses as well as any book. She knew what Lucky needed was someone genuine and so steady that he'd have to believe in them even if he didn't believe in himself. But that person had to also be physically unintimidating. He himself was quite small and adults were a bigger physical threat. That's where I came in. My mother trusted me to be Lucky's someone and as it turned out, so did he. Like any good relationship in the human world, our bond took time and patience. We moved at his pace, step by step, until the day came when Lucky allowed me to brush him fully for the first time. I felt like I had been given the whole candy store and the comfort that radiated from him as he leaned into the brush was the best reward I could have imagined.

As Lucky began to heal, both physically and emotionally, it became clear he was ready for the next chapter in his life. He had put on weight, his coat shone with a hint of vibrancy, and his eyes no longer held that haunted look of a horse who's forgotten what kindness is.

Eventually, a kind couple with a quiet farm offered to take him in. On the day of his departure, I got the honor of leading him from the trailer to his new shed and removing his brand new royal blue halter. As the adults stood around chatting, I watched Lucky explore his new surroundings, sniffing the dirt, rich hay and full water trough with thorough curiosity.

When the conversation lulled and everyone wandered out of the shed, leaving Lucky and me alone for a moment, something unexpected happened. Lucky walked over, lowered his head, and bit me right on the shoulder. I was stunned, the sharp pain bringing tears to my eyes. My initial reaction was confusion and hurt. Why would he do that? I had worked so hard to help him, and now he was turning on me?

My mother rushed over, and seeing my distressed face, she gently explained that it wasn't a bite out of anger or aggression. It was a "love nip," as she called it – a gesture horses often use when grooming one another to show affection and acceptance. In his own way, Lucky was telling me that he saw me as part of his herd, that I was someone he trusted and cared for; and while I'm not in any way encouraging allowing horses to bite, that day marked one of my first lessons in herd communication and understanding a horse's language beyond what you can learn from any training book.

Lucky taught me what it means to build a partnership, a bond that transcends commands and obedience. He showed me that trust, once given, is something precious and worth protecting. I loved Lucky, and Lucky loved me. Through him, I learned what it means to cross that delicate line between training and true partnership; something that would shape the way I approached horses for years to come.

{Chapter 3}

Rescue Overflows - Cicero and Figaro

It was springtime. A time for new life, for adventures and hope in the future as the world is reborn. The first tulips were popping their heads out at the end of long wind whipped stems. The last of the frost had gone, and life was busy around the farm. Our German Shepherd had just had an accidental litter of pups with a neighbor's boxer, and the neighbors' swans were determined to build their nest in the lilac bushes along our property. Our horses got a lot of desensitization to the honking, flapping, cantankerous birds that year.

These weren't the only wild things happening though. A local rescue had an overflow of horses. They asked my mother to go and try to purchase a couple of horses to remove them from the complicated situation they were currently in. This was the 90s, and there weren't as many formal, well-funded rescues as there are now. There was only so much space and so many resources. But when you needed someone good with animals, and you needed someone who couldn't say no when horses needed help - you called my mom.

Cicero, a liver chestnut Morab mare and Figaro, a grey aged Arabian gelding were a package deal. They came with an unlikely third companion: an exasperating little black and tan pygmy goat whose personality couldn't have been further from her sweet name—Cookie.

We had a feeding arrangement for several days on the property they were all originally housed on. They had been sheltered together in a small shed, and it wasn't long before we realized Cookie was trouble.

Despite the innocent-sounding name, she was far from a gentle creature. She was rotund, stubborn, and, to put it bluntly, not the ideal introduction to goat ownership for first timers like us. Cicero was in decent health apart from her feet and teeth which were badly neglected. She was young and judging by what remained of a fat crest still on her neck, had likely been quite hefty at one time. It was Figaro who left us speechless. He was the skinniest horse I had ever seen and quite aged. From the first time we fed the horses we saw an issue. Cookie would lower her head and, with surprising strength for her size, ram the horses' knees and faces in a bid to snatch up whatever measly bits of hay she could get her teeth on. Watching her relentlessly charge at the horses, I couldn't help but feel a mixture of irritation and pity. Her antics might have been amusing under different circumstances and with a wooden post as a recipient. Considering how little food there had recently been to go around, I understood her desperation, but it didn't make her any less of a menace. I couldn't help but cringe each time she rammed a knee, or got too close to an eye as the horses ate.

As for Figaro, his good nature was turning into his downfall as the young, hardy and aggressive animals were winning, and he was starving. His pelvis no longer held any muscles or fat to round what should have been beautiful Arabian curves. His scapulas were visible and clearly defined rather than blending into the bulk of an elegant shoulder. His ribcage shown like a skeletal anatomy model; the ribs jutting out from his sides like the keys of an old piano, and his entire frame seemed to sag under the weight of exhaustion and neglect. But his eyes were the worst. This precious souls hope, his light, was gone. I remember being unsure if he would make it through the trailer ride home. Blessedly he did, and once he was there, we moved to the next test, would he make it through the night after the stress of being moved? What about the next day? We made an emergency call to our vet and had both horses scheduled to be seen as soon as possible as we settled them into their new temporary home.

Bringing a new horse is often a fun, exciting experience; but approaching a barn the morning after you bring home an animal in that kind of shape is a daunting experience. You don't know what may be waiting for you.

Morning broke, and my mother and I took our walk to the far side of the property and the little antique carriage house we had designated for quarantine for the new arrivals. One of us clicked our tongue to call the horses and waited. Out strutted Cookie from her little side pen, like the queen of the roost, small tendrils of hay still draped out the side of her mouth as she chomped greedily. Cicero was next, bright and sunshiny emerging with a happy whinny to us as she stepped out of her stall and into the retreating morning fog. Then there was a pause. A terrible pause so loaded with hope and fear. Silence reigned as no further noises came from Figaro's section of the shed as we approached. I remember saying some less than publicly acceptable words, regardless of how appropriate the sentiment was at the time. Then with a peace and grace only age can bring, a grey face emerged from the darkness of the shed, covered in shavings. Figaro bobbed his head up and down at us as if to say "Finally you're here. Get with more food!" It was a happy teary breakfast as we sat in the shed with Figaro in a section all his own, where the extra deep bedding we had added the night before had clearly been gratefully utilized and fed him his mornings soaked mash.

At the vet check, we learned that other than his weight, Figaro was in decent shape. His body would take time to heal, but his organs sounded alright despite the neglect. His eyes were brighter already after just a couple days, and he walked slowly around his pen nibbling at the free choice of hay and loose mineral salt now available to him. As part of his care his teeth were addressed, the few that were left, and his feet had been trimmed to a neat healthy length.

When he was finally well enough to move with Cicero to the larger pasture out front, it took another few weeks for cars to stop slowing down by our property to gawk. He was cared for, and he was eating. But weight takes time, and in the meantime, he was making his way back through the journey of weight gain, most of which looked various levels of terrible. During this time, we were getting lots of well-meaning questions from passersby. The 90s were a little different in that way than today. If people had a problem, they would stop at your house and speak to you about it. We had many inquiries on why we had such a skinny horse but after a bit of explaining that you don't just hide him in the back until he's 'appealing to look at' folks would offer to help with him. They wanted to stay to brush him, to pet him, or even to help pay for his feed. So many offered any goodness they could to contribute to his journey to wellness and help repair the damage. I miss those innocent days when people were more understanding, and more giving.

As for Cicero, we were able to hunt down her

backstory to an out of state public trail riding facility. She was ridable, and in good health but sorely lacked skills. For those who have never been on a public trail ride horse, they most typically are in a perpetual game of follow the leader. Taught to put their head down and follow the horses' tail in front of them while toting a tourist safely on their backs. Theres nothing inherently wrong with this training; it serves its purpose, but it is sometimes difficult to unzombie the horse or get it to have a mind of its own when you first tell it "Yes! You can even go over there by yourself!" Cicero lacked confidence to navigate her world without a tail in front of her face to follow. So, as spring gave way to the golden touch of summer, our feeding and training work settled into an easy rhythm.

It's been a little while, hasn't it? I bet you've been wondering about Cookie the goat. Miss her, did you? No? Well, honestly, neither did we. Cookie had a personality that could fill a barn—and not always in the best way.

After a lot of consideration, we decided it was time for her to move on to greener pastures—literally.

We loaded Cookie into the back of our brand-new seafoam green Oldsmobile Silhouette minivan, secured her with a few hay bales, and hit the road. Off we went, scouting the countryside for a farm that would welcome her ....spirited nature.

We found Cookie a new home with a kind, older gentleman who had a small herd of goats and plenty of space for her to roam. I'd wager that this man had never experienced what amounted to a drive-by goat-ing. After knocking on his door and inquiring on his interest in a new family member, that's essentially what happened!

It didn't take long for Cookie to start exploring her new surroundings, and as we drove away, we knew we'd made the right choice for everyone involved.

With Cookie settled into her new home and our farm feeling a little quieter, we turned our focus back to our horses. Because we'd purchased the horses privately, we had the flexibility to rehome or sell them as we saw fit. It was a relief to be able to consider what was best for each horse, and we hoped to ensure they found owners who would truly appreciate their unique personalities and needs. Cicero had an opinion all her own now and could be ridden absent another horse. She was a fine mare with lovely gaits, a hazelnut-colored coat, strong build, and enough personality to launch a rocket ship if friendliness could be used as fuel. A first-time horse owner family member of mine bought Cicero. However, after a few months with a steep learning curve, decided horse life was not for them. And so, she was returned to our care. I adored Cicero. We rode along all the local country roads, discovered many new places together, dipped our toes into barrel racing, and went on some great adventures. We were a great match – personality wise. The unfortunate thing about Cicero in my case was her size, or lack thereof. It is a common rule of thumb that a rider and their saddle should not exceed twenty percent of the horse's bodyweight. There are multiple other factors to consider as well such as balance of the rider, breed of horse, age, and the saddle and tack. However, at the time I wasn't done growing, and I was already past her limit without a saddle. She was far too small for me to continue riding her long term, so I began the search for another home with a properly sized rider.

Figaro's story is one that took turn after turn. Not all for the better. We had high hopes for his future when we found a new home for him. The buyer was a woman and her young son, and on paper, it seemed perfect. They had a small, private barn with a lean-to shelter, no competition for food, and a child to dote on him. It sounded like the ideal place for Figaro to thrive, so on delivery day, we loaded him into the trailer, feeling a mix of sadness and optimism over his moving on. He had become a part of the family, and we had connected heart and soul with this gentle treasure as he became well over the previous months. After arriving, we unloaded Figaro, took possession of the check, and asked to see where he'd be staying.

The place was an older farmhouse with original outbuildings in need of some repair, not unlike ours. The peeling paint and sagging wood were signs of age, but not necessarily neglect we understood. We knew firsthand that horses didn't need a show barn or luxury amenities to be happy and healthy. So, we still held hope as we followed the path back to a barn where they planned to house him.

That's where things went south.

The shelter was inadequate in the best term, his bedding was insufficient, and worse, the area was littered with dangers. Sharp metal feed troughs, broken glass, and rusted nails were scattered around the barn and the holding pen where he was meant to be confined. More rusty nails, and metal wire spiked outward from the walls in easy reach. Boards hung from the ceiling precariously and the whole structure leaned at an extremely concerning angle. It was a nightmare we hadn't seen coming. With a shared look we came to the same conclusion. He could not stay here.

My mother attempted to explain to them that this was not a proper safe place for Figaro and that we could not allow him to stay here with the hazards. We offered the check back and kindly attempted to collect him from them again. A great many curse words were thrown at us for this observation. And we were told to leave the property. Things escalated quickly from there.

Panicked, we called the local authorities to ask for advice, hoping there was some way they could intervene and bring Figaro back home. But there was nothing to be done. The sale was final, and legally when money changed hands in the driveway, Figaro belonged to new owners. I still remember that sickening feeling of realization—like the floor had been ripped out from under me. This was one of our first sales ever, and we hadn't yet learned the hard lesson: never finalize a deal without thoroughly inspecting where the horse will live if you get the chance, no matter how trustworthy the buyer seems. As heartbreaking as it was to accept, Figaro was out of our hands and authorities did not step in to help.

Desperate to remedy our mistake, we immediately requested again of the buyer to let us take him home and offered to buy him back for more than they paid us, but they refused. They said he was fine, that they would make do, that we were overreacting. In a last-ditch effort, we asked to stay, and help them make this area as safe as it could be. There was nothing we could do at that point but try to make the place more suitable. Begrudgingly they agreed and scowling at us most of the time, we spent hours pulling out nails, sweeping up glass, and moving the sharp metal feed troughs, our eyes stinging with tears as we worked. I remember Figaro watching us, his gaze steady and patient, as if trying to reassure us that it would be okay.

We worked until after dark and the drive home that evening was unbearable. Tears poured down my cheeks the entire way, and I felt crushed under the weight of guilt and helplessness. We had sold him into this. We hadn't done enough.

Over the next few weeks, we called the family occasionally, hoping they would change their minds and agree to sell him back. Each time, the answer was the same— "No. He's ours now." I begged the local authorities to do a welfare check, but I was turned down again and again. Each rejection deepened the pit in my stomach.

I spent countless nights over those few weeks lying awake, replaying the day we left Figaro over and over again. I would lie in bed, staring at the ceiling, wondering if he was okay, if he was being fed properly, or if he was scared and confused about what he had done to be put back into a situation of scarce food and poor shelter. The sense of helplessness was suffocating, and it felt like mourning a loved one who had disappeared without a trace. The only difference was I knew exactly where he last was—I just couldn't reach him. Despite our calls, pleas, and offers, there was nothing we could do. Figaro's fate was out of our hands, and the weight of that reality was crushing.

Each time, we picked up the phone and dialed their number, hearts pounding in our chests and each time our call was met with a firm often rude rejection. During the fourth week, I tried again, but the line just rang and rang. The same thing happened the next day. And the day after that. With each unanswered call, the pit in my stomach deepened. What if something had happened to him? What if he'd been sold off to someone else, lost again in a sea of unfamiliar faces? Perhaps that would have been better, a new place could be better right? Not knowing was unbearable.

By the time another week had passed, we were convinced we'd lost Figaro forever. We mourned him like he was truly gone—grieving not just for the horse, but for the opportunity we'd let slip through our fingers to protect him, to bring him home, and for the failure we had executed. It was a hard lesson to learn, and one that came with a hefty emotional price.

If there's one thing, I hope readers take away from Figaro's story, it's this: never rush a sale. Never finalize a deal without seeing firsthand where your horse will be living, and above all, trust your gut. Horses can't speak for themselves, and once money changes hands, it's often too late to turn back. I wish I'd known that back then. But all I can do now is share Figaro's story and hope others won't make the same mistake.

There is, however, a second lesson I want to share from Figaro's story: that even in the darkest moments, there is always a sliver of hope.

A few days after the phone stopped ringing endlessly—after the ringing silence became a symbol of everything we feared, I made one last call. I hesitated before dialing, not wanting to hear that same repetitive tone. But this time, the receiver on the other end picked up.

It was not the original buyers, but a family member. The details are a blur now, but I'll never forget the basis of what they told us. The woman who had purchased Figaro had passed away unexpectedly. Her partner, who had been away on long-haul trucking routes, had arrived home to a horse he had no idea they owned, or any idea how to care for. In the midst of grieving, he had reached out to a local barn, asking if they could take Figaro.

The barn, reputable and known for their quality of care, went out to see Figaro. They loved his gentle nature and took him in without hesitation. Although the circumstances which caused this relocation were incredibly sad, the sense of relief for Figaro's situation was like a gust of air in a stifling room. We asked for the barn's name and immediately made the call to check on his situation.

The owners of the barn were warm and understanding, sharing with us everything they knew about Figaro's weeks at the farmhouse. He'd only been with their facility for a few days, but they could already tell he was special. The barn had a riding lesson program and once he was healthier, they hoped he could be a part of it if he was ridable. The children at the barn had already taken a liking to him, brushing him and feeding him treats every day. They were moved by his story and glad to have some background information and invited us to visit the barn. It felt like a dream. Figaro recognized us right away, lifting his head and giving a familiar head toss and soft nicker. His eyes were brighter and calmer than I'd expected. He was in a spacious, clean stall with plenty of hay, fresh water and a big pile of shavings to rest on. He had lost some weight again during his time at the farmhouse, but they were working diligently to get him back on track. We spent hours talking to the barn owners, sharing Figaro's history, and marveling at the love he now received from a gaggle of giggling children. The guilt and heartbreak we'd carried for weeks started to evaporate off us like steam. Knowing he was finally in a place where he would be loved and cared for brought an inexplicable sense of peace.

Standing in the barn aisle, watching Figaro munch contentedly on a flake of leafy alfalfa hay, I knew we'd been given a second chance - one we maybe didn't deserve for our initial ignorance, but were grateful for nonetheless. Despite everything that happened, Figaro had found his way to a place he truly deserved, where he would be appreciated for who he was. His journey taught me that hope isn't always about getting back what you lost - it's about finding a way forward, even when you think you've reached the story's end.

Back at home, Cicero continued to make progress advancing in her riding. She was such a delight to work with every time. However, her size was still an issue for our long-term partnership. Eventually we located a larger horse I had a great deal of interest in for barrel racing. You'll read his story in a later chapter. Cicero was exactly what the sellers wanted for their upcoming move to Colorado. She was pretty! She was smart! You could ride her with only a hula-hoop!

It was a trade. My little rescue mare went off to her new future westbound herding cows. One last word about Cookie. After a very excited phone call from the gentleman we rehomed her to, it turns out she wasn't just carrying some extra weight. She was in fact carrying around four tiny bouncing extra weights. I was so glad they were bouncing around his property and not mine

– I should really stick to horses.

{Chapter 4}

Spots – Cassie

Some people can make any horse crazy. I have seen
it time and time again. Whether it be with good or
poor intent towards the horse, there are some folks
who cause themselves more grief than happiness
with even the smallest, least threatening animal. My
mother had a mare - Jazz, who you will read about
later in this book - who we had agreed to trade for a
foal. We located a seller who had two fillies
available. One a sorrel Quarter Horse, and one
tricolor tobiano Paint. The day of the trade came
and when the trailer arrived, the driver backed it up
directly to our round pen without us indicating

where to park. My mother and I exchanged questioning glances, shrugged it off and approached the back of the trailer as the owners disembarked the truck. The woman selling the fillies reached the back of the trailer with a limp and sporting a sling on one arm. We said our hellos and found ourselves instantly regaled with the tale of tales involving the meanest horse to ever walk the earth, the Paint filly she had brought with her that day. She indicated the ultra-sweet natured sorrel filly was just inside the door of the trailer and she would let her out because we probably didn't want the other one as it was vicious. She indicated how glad she was she had put her in the front slot with a full wall divider in the trailer which contained her.

The fillies had come from a feed lot a few weeks earlier and been in a pen with a number of other horses. At the lot, she said that the staff would throw feed in the middle of the pen over the fence and the crowded pen of horses would fight for dominance for a chance at food.

This filly was in that pen for a couple of weeks she had calculated before she purchased her. A few days before bringing the two babies to our home, the woman had attempted to corral the fillies into a stall. In a normally logical thought process, she employed the use of grain to lure the uncertain babies into the space.

The problem was the Paint filly associated that sound with being battered and having to fight for herself. So, when the woman rattled grain inside the stall, the little filly had kicked the dickens out of her, resulting in the injuries now on display and a new cruel name for the poor thing.

Now, I understand being cautious around a horse. I understand injury, fear, and pain from a horse related incident. So, I do not judge this woman on her feelings, but the showmanship of it was really something. She first opened the back trailer door and let out the little sorrel filly; giving her a gentle pat as she exited the door. She was a good size, with a nice round hip, attractive head, and good solid build. Sweet as could be, and calm to boot in a new place. She walked around my round pen searching for things to nibble. We agreed she was lovely but indicated we would still like to see the other one, so we knew we made the right choice. While I offered to go in and unlock the trailer divider in the front section for the nervous woman, she indicated she didn't want a lawsuit if that 'little monster' did it to me too before our trade was complete. She entered the trailer slowly. It was bright outside, and the inside of the trailer was quite dark, casting an air of mystery over the whole situation as we squinted towards the door. We heard the lock to the divider slide back.

Almost immediately following the click, and thud of the divider finding its home along the far wall, the woman rocketed from the trailer at superhuman speed and yelled

"Get back, stay back!" to my mother and I. She immediately scooted from the pen via the closest panel and told us she would feel better if we did too.

We declined to leave, waiting to see what would step from the trailer.

At first, there was no movement and all was quiet. Then slowly, dainty hoofbeats tiptoed from the front of the trailer. In the door appeared the horse the owner had named after a certain childhood villainous figure with a penchant for spotted fur and a cold-hearted demeanor.

You have probably seen those old cartoons where a character sees something they fall in love with instantly. The music swells in the background, and hearts and starbursts float from the characters wide eyes in utter disbelief of a love so true, so instant, so pure. My mother and I were cast as the main characters in this episode, and utterly melted upon watching the petite little filly pause at the edge of the trailer to greet the wide world. She seemed unsure if she should step down into the round pen or stay safely on the trailer edge. Her darling build was night and day from the attractively bulky form of the other filly even though they were both only four months old.

Making the decision to step down into the dirt, she wobbled a little on her delicate legs after the long ride and stood looking at us uncertainly. It was then that I did something that made the owner's face contort in terror. I sat down right in the filly's path.

I'm not a complete idiot, I promise, but there are times you just know. I had heard her story, and I was certain this was simply a misunderstood defense mechanism that happened to be associated with something that is normally a horse's favorite thing - grain. Since I had none, and there was nothing around which would sound similar, I took the chance on being correct.

After a long moment, she ambled across the twenty or so feet between us and placed her tiny inquiring nose, little nostrils flaring, into my awaiting palms. She was small, warm, and velveteen to touch, everything a person thinks of when they think of a baby. In her bright eyes I saw she was kind and there was no way we could take the sorrel filly as ours. My mother was of the same opinion.

The 'little villain' lost her cruel name that day and became forever more known as Cassie. She was the first baby I had the joy of being involved in raising, and from that moment on, she became the little light of our farm.

Watching Cassie grow into a fine, strong mare over the next two and a half years was one of the most rewarding experiences of my life. Through gentle training paired with her kind nature, she developed a calm and level adult temperament. She took all things in stride and even her greatest challenges were met with a look of trust and gentleness in her eyes that touched our hearts deeply.

When Cassie came of age and was still too small for either my mother or me to safely ride, one of my very best friends put the first ride on her back. As was her nature, Cassie didn't put a single hoof out of line. She took to having a rider on her back as if she'd been doing it all her life, a true natural who instantly enjoyed having a partnership with people. We took her to her first parades with all their chaotic, jumbled noises and flashing lights. Despite older, more experienced horses sometimes having a difficult time, she never once balked or hesitated. Cassie just moved with a grace and confidence that made us all incredibly proud. She was a special mare, a rare soul fueled by the unwavering trust she placed in those who cared for her.

Our plan was always to keep Cassie. But as the years went by and she grew, then stopped growing, we were not able to ride her without putting her small frame in danger of overexertion. We considered finding a trainer to teach her to pull a cart, turning her into a fancy trick horse with her bows, maybe teaching her to count and to smile, but fate has this beautiful way of helping many people with one blessing.

Not long after we had discussed our options for Cassie to have a full life of activities and having a job, a woman stopped by our farm. It was quite unexpected, but she expressed to my mother that her best friend had passed away a couple of years earlier. She had been in a dark place, as is bound to happen with such loss. Here's the kicker – Cassie was her best friend. Not in a "I like that horse" way but in a drive by every day and see her and just 'know' she's meant to be with you way.

Take the leap with me here even if you're not typically this type of person. Personally, I believe in all sorts of 'magic', and this was just one of those times when things are brought together for a special reason that heals many. Call it God, call it fate, call it chance or luck or whatever you wish but there is something out there that is better than we are at arranging, loving, and guiding a great many beautiful things.

I truly believe we were Cassies keepers and were meant to get her through to her next stop along the way regardless of what our initial plans were. Her life was here to heal her new owner's heart.

We connected every year with her owners at an

annual horse fair and received updates through email and texts for her whole life. Cassies first saddle, her first rider, her first trail ride. We were 'there' when she met her barn buddy, when she got a new barn to live in at home with her people, and even when things got tough.

A few years ago, I received word that Cassie's health was failing, and that her time was coming to an end. While it's heartbreaking to know that she's no longer with us, there is something truly magical about being connected to an animal its whole life through. It's comforting to know that, thanks to a seemingly chance encounter, Cassie spent her days in a place that felt like heaven on earth for her. She never knew a day of want or sorrow with her owners—only love, companionship, and joy.

I'm endlessly grateful to Cassie's final owners—who I know will recognize themselves in these words. Thank you for giving her a life full of love and meaning. You are truly wonderful, and I know Cassie's spirit is forever grateful too.

{Chapter 5}

Spot the Difference – Zee

This story is different from the others in this book. While I learn something from every horse, and I hope every horse learns something from me, in all honesty, he probably didn't learn a single thing from me. But I owe Zee everything. I owe my continued love of horses, and my career with horses, to this gelding. By association then, most horses in this book owe their time with me to him as well.

My mother purchased Zee for me when I was about ten following my getting badly hurt in a horse incident on another horse. I had entirely sworn off horses for months following the healing process of a jammed back, broken ankle and completely shattered confidence. He was a dreamboat for most horse people. The Rolls-Royce of mounts. A fifteen two hand loud grey roan and white blanket appaloosa, in his prime, with a show record pages and pages long. He had every fancy button one could install, and he was incredibly well cared for his whole life at an upscale barn. My mother had gone to see a kid safe leopard appaloosa originally; knowing it was my favorite coat pattern and hoping it would entice me back on a horse.

She ended up with Zee after falling in love with him at first sight. A mother's intuition. The seller informed her he was "not exactly on the same budget point as the other horse and far above where she had indicated she wanted to be for this purchase". So, we were poor after she bought him, but sure had a nice horse.

Now, one would think of having the high-end show horse with the dream coat and the personality to go with it as the best fortune ever. Folks, I kid you not, I hated him.

There was no way around it. As a young kid with minimal refined training riding a show trained horse whose cues were ultra refined was a challenging return to riding. I could not make this animal go forward, turn, or listen to me in any way apart from just putting up with me as I tried to communicate.

One of the first days I returned to the barn we took lessons at, he proceeded to back up all the way up the mountain of shavings in the corner of the arena with me aboard, embarrassing me terribly in front of my riding friends. I continued to work with him - let's be honest, he continued to grace me with allowing me to work with him- for several weeks at the behest of my mother and her empty pocketbook. Eventually I got with the program, and we began working as a team.

At local shows Zee was a super star, English or Western, bareback or riding double, he brought my riding skills and my confidence along in great measure. Even when things didn't go to plan, or we didn't win the blue ribbon, I had my best friend by my side, and that was all that really mattered. It wasn't all show glamor and groomed lessons, there were a few times our partnership didn't go as planned. I believe I came off of Zee more than any other horse to date, and it was never once his fault. The few times I attempted to learn to mount bareback, I either splatted up against his side like a Looney Toons character or just flew over him instead – one time even landing in our lilac bushes on the far side. I remember his side eye looks that seemed to say, 'what on earth is this child doing now?" We went through the tandem bareback class practice and hit the sand a few times with our partners as well.

In the sandy raked arena of lessons and shows was not the only place he was sure to take good care of me. We trail rode quite a bit and had our share of adventures over the years.

There was one instance in which Zee met his match and calm was no longer part of his playbook. One summer a friend of mine asked that I go riding with her family. I was thrilled to go somewhere with a group. When they arrived, huge trailer in tow, I was shocked to find that only the smallest section of the very back was for horses. The front had all been modified into a camper. They opened the back door to reveal their three horses' side to side looking not unlike a can of sardines. Strange horses, small spaces, strange request, but Zee loaded into the compact space stepping sideways up when asked and let the door close anyways, something few horses I know would have tolerated.

Upon arrival at the beautiful riding park, we unloaded the horses. Zee seemed to have had a perfectly calm trip and was unflustered. The front horse in the bunch however was unsound after the ride. Kathys parents chose to stay at the trailer and relax due to the lame horse while Kathy and I went out on our own adventure. All of Kathys horses were gaited, and much faster than Zee. It took a good amount of coaxing to get him to extend his walks and trots to keep up. After all, he was a show ring low and slow kind of guy! As young daredevils do when unsupervised, we took some risks. We traded horses for a bit so I could ride the gaited horse in its special saddle, and she could ride bareback on what was according to her "the slowest horse in the world". God bless him Zee was anything but fast or urgent, as a lot of Appaloosas I have owned seem to be. Eventually the scenery lost its intrigue, and we decided to play hide and seek on horseback.

While looking for Kathy, Zee and I found a beautiful creek. Shallow but running at the bottom of a relatively steep slope on either side going up or coming down. Zee made it across in his dependable easy going way; and we made our way down the trail still in search of our friend. As we approached a dead end to the trail, there the grass grew tall and the trees grew tighter, I applauded Kathys ability to hide a relatively good-sized horse from sight. Her mare would not stand out as much with her Sorrel coat as Zee would with his black and white polk-adot coat in a natural setting but still, hiding a horse in the wide open? I gently pulled Zee to a whoa to ponder which wrong turn we had taken in my search. Just as the grass a ways into the brush started moving, and whatever it was, it was coming towards us. What a clever person Kathy was I thought. Hiding her horse and coming back to creep up.

"Kathy! I can see you" I laughed. But the motion kept coming towards us.

"I found you; you lose!" I proclaimed. Zee started to paw the ground under me. Then began a prancing in place he had never done, starting to turn back down the trail.

"Ok enough you're scaring Zee" I said. "Not funny anymore Kathy" Zee took one lurch forward down the trail. Mercifully I was able to pull him up and stay on his back as I turned us back toward the grass. Just as I did, a giant snarling raccoon erupted from the thick brush. In that moment, my soul left my body, and Zee erupted into the fastest horse in existence. He rocketed back down the trail and leapt cleanly across the creek. What a wild ride. It was my first time jumping a horse bareback and despite the utter fear we were being chased; it was a rush like no other.

We tore back down the trail and to the main branch where it had split off. Back through the lines of trees, and past the turn off to the trailer. What a ride. Zee finally agreed to stop in a clearing on the other side of the small trailer area. He stopped with no snorting or ceremony and simply stood, content we were away from harm. It was then I looked up to see my friends horse tied to a nearby tree. She greeted me with more snark than I was in the mood for considering the ride I had just taken

"There you are, I was about to change roles and come looking for you instead."

I could write a whole book about Zee alone. Never has another horse brought me back from the brink of giving up my horse dream quite so thoroughly. Zee's time with me came to an end a couple of summers after Buck arrived on the scene. It wasn't the ending I had hoped for, but sometimes things don't go as planned. There are horses who bond deeply with each other, forming inseparable friendships, and others who simply coexist without fuss; and then, there are pairs like Zee and Buck—opposites who couldn't find common ground no matter how hard I tried. Zee despised Buck immediately upon his arrival. They were across the barn aisle from each other, which should have been more than enough room to mind their own business. But like that coworker who annoys us just by existing in the same office, Buck was mortal enemy number one. Zee would kick at his stall walls and pace angrily, and despite our best efforts refused to stop. There had been plenty of horses who didn't get along right away come through our herd and with separate turnout, and everyone getting attention and good food, the storm always blew over quickly. This time was different. Over time, the constant recurring jolt of kicking lead to a heartbreaking injury in Zee's hind legs.

Our care team did everything they could to rehabilitate him, holding on to hope that he'd bounce back, but after months of care and watching him struggle when going back to work, it became clear that he would never again be able to support my weight for riding. The reality of his retirement weighed heavily on my heart, not because he was getting older, but because I could see the light dimming in his eyes. He wasn't the same Zee who had spent his life showing, trailering to new adventures, and working with children. He was becoming depressed. His spirit, once so full of life and energy, now seemed lost and distant.

I knew I had to do something, something more than just offering him a pasture to stand in. Zee needed a purpose, someone to bond with, and something to look forward to every day. So, I started looking for a new home for him, a place where he could continue doing what he loved, even if I couldn't be the one sharing those experiences with him. I reached out to different barns and trainers, inquiring about weight limits and possibilities for him as a child's mount. I wanted him to have the little girl he so deserved. When I finally found a family who felt like the perfect fit, it was both a relief and a heartbreak. They had everything I wanted for him: a cozy small farm, excellent care, and—most importantly—a little girl who was over the moon to have him. The night they took him home I received a photo that made me cry with joy. It seemed an unassuming photo to most, I am sure. His new little girl stood there holding his lead rope, her little blonde bob cut framing a beaming face. And as for Zee, he stood with his neck lowered, his nose touching the front of her shirt as if he was cuddling her, and his eyes were so full of peace I hadn't seen in months.

Seeing Zee settle into his new role filled me with bittersweet joy. He transformed back into his old self almost immediately, the sparkle in his eyes returning in every photo I saw as he carted his new princess around the show ring. They were a picture of grace and partnership, and I was told stories of how they collected ribbons and trophies together—proof of the happiness he'd found in his new home. Years later, when his rider had outgrown him, Zee was leased to a tiny three-year-old down the road. This proud old horse, with all his experience, took on the task of teaching her to ride too, carrying her with care and gentleness as if she were made of porcelain.

For the rest of his days, Zee remained a source of joy, helping one child after another find their confidence and love for horses. He truly flourished, thriving as the beloved steed of little girls who needed a wise, steady presence in their lives. In his twenty-six years, Zee blessed everyone he met, and knowing he found his purpose again after leaving me is a comfort I'll always hold dear despite never quite stopping missing him or filling the hole left by his absence.

I like to think that some horses are meant to be teachers, and that's exactly what Zee was. He gave everything he had to the people who needed him, and I'll forever be grateful that he spent some time and shared some of that soul with me in my time of need through those fragile years learning to love and trust again, and that Zee ended his life in a place where he was valued and loved for the remarkable horse he was. Sometimes all we need is a steady gentle guardian, and a mother who knows what's best for us, to show us the world is still a safe place to dream.

{Chapter 6}

That's Gonna Leave a Mark – Telemark Jazz

Red mares. Oh, the stories, memes, and jokes that circulate in the horse industry about the Chestnuts and the Sorrels of the female type. From a young age, I remember knowing even from the classic Black Beauty books and movies that the red mare was fiery, and beautiful, but mean spirited.

Jazz was as red as they come and upon first glance in her story, she seemed to pretty well fit the bill. But by the end of her story, I'll let you decide whether these labels are fair judgments or harmful generalizations - ones that result in misunderstood behavior being unfairly blamed on a horse's coat color.

Jazzy's shining coat reflected like flames glow in the dark. She was an American Saddlebred with a pedigree to die for, and movement that would have won her a lifetime of blue ribbons. She was the kind of beautiful that made the flowers turn their faces to watch with envy as she passed. The problem then? She was aggressive. Jazz was so aggressive in fact; she would be turned out and the door locked so they could clean her stall. She had a pristine stall, the best food, and people who loved her but were terrified. It seemed her aggression was worse towards men than women, and worse towards dark haired people than light haired. We took Jazz on believing – not through lies, or deception, but honesty by the sellers and hope on our parts – that social time with other horses, and more grass and space, would help her level out.

My family owned Jazz for several years. She was Cicero's best friend while they resided in our pasture and loved Rocket with all her marish heart. We allowed her a

good amount of time to just be a horse, and I wish I could say things were quiet but there wouldn't be much of a story here if they had been. Jazzy spent her days eating with our other horses, basking in the sunshine, and come feeding time, attacking anyone who wasn't my mother. My father, my brother and I were all subject to near daily shoulder bites, attempted face bites, trampling, and kicks, or attempts at any artful combination of the three. My mother, in all her 'good with any animal to walk the earth glory', never was around when Jazz did any of these incriminating behaviors. It was as if the horse was not only targeting people, but careful not to be caught by the one person she actually liked.

Jazzy's previous owners had seen the vet about her behavior, and it had been labeled hormonal "mareish" behavior that 'some mares just have.' After a while we began to want a second opinion on that statement. It was time Jazzy started being considered for other issues than needing time with a herd, needing time out just being a horse, needing a new environment etc. So, we called the vet in our area for a health evaluation of the behaviors.

They checked her back and legs for soreness, her teeth for sharp points and her mouth for sores. She had a thorough going over for pain spots, and flexion of her neck and limbs. The result? "We have ruled out pain. Maybe she just needs to work her mind more, she needs a job."

A job was not something I was looking forward to doing with Jazz. We had worked at round penning a few times and I was not her favorite person to be within a hundred yards of, so climbing aboard sounded about as appealing as chewing on tinfoil.

A week later as I figuratively chewed on metal and prayed, I climbed aboard her with my mother holding the lead rope in hopes she would behave in front of her favorite person. My mother had recently undergone surgery which forced her to take a break from riding so was forced into the position of helper, rather than rider.

Jazz, I suppose, in choosing to only repeatedly bite the air in a constant tooth snapping action, stomping ferociously, and looking much like something straight from Hell below, counts vs actually killing me, did pretty well.

You don't know what you don't know. At that time in our lives, no one knew nearly as much as they do today about equine ulcers. Looking back, I have to remind myself to forgive the ignorance we faced— not just from our own lack of knowledge but also from what we were never told by the professionals we trusted. The gaps in understanding weren't intentional, but it's hard not to feel frustrated knowing that better information might have changed the course of things sooner. In the end, it wasn't a vet or specialist who put us on the right track. It was our farrier, an observant man who'd seen more horses than most, who first suggested the possibility of ulcers.

At the time, the idea seemed almost laughable to us. We'd chalked up Jazzy's escalating aggression to a behavioral problem, something that could be fixed with training, or, at worst, was just a part of her personality we'd have to accept. After all, she was a fiery mare, and people always say red mares are more difficult, don't they?

But as her outbursts grew more frequent and more dangerous, the farrier's words came back to haunt us. What if we were missing something? What if this wasn't just attitude? We reached out to the vet again, hesitantly suggesting the possibility of ulcers. There was some hemming and hawing on their end, as if we were being silly to consider it.

"Could be ulcers," they finally allowed, "but it's just as likely she's just being a mare." We'd heard that before. Every behavior issue seemed to get dismissed as just "mareishness." But something in Jazzy's eyes was different. She wasn't just being difficult. She was desperate, angry, in a way that spoke of pain, not defiance.

"What's the worst that could happen if we treat her as if she has ulcers?" my mother asked. It wasn't an unreasonable question. The treatment would be costly, sure, and it would throw off our barn routine, since we'd have to separate her for medications daily. But what was a little extra inconvenience when the stakes were so high? I was willing to try anything to save her, to help her. If it turned out we were wrong, well, we'd be out a bit of money and time. But if we were right? If ulcers were the root of her behavior? We might have a chance at learning for the first time who Jazz really was underneath the pain. With our decision made, we set out to alter her diet and begin treatment. We introduced the medications and feeding schedule recommended for ulcer management. She was kept on a strict regimen of small, frequent meals, plenty of forage, and ulcer medication. We wanted to believe it would work. But Jazzy didn't understand what we were trying to do. She only knew that her world was changing again, and not all of it felt good. We let her rejoin the herd at night after her day feedings were over. Then, in the midst of all these adjustments, there was an incident that made my heart drop. I often took treats to the horses while they were out grazing. It was a common occurrence, and they were all very used to my presence. However, the day I took apples out, I checked where Jazz was as I usually did, then proceeded to start feeding the close horses who were safer. I was standing well over two hundred feet away when Jazzy, without warning, charged across the paddock, hooves pounding the earth like a freight train. She neighed at me, which was new, and I like a young ignorant teen, though perhaps she felt better and wanted to participate, after all, my heart horse often did the same when coming to greet me. So, I stood there a little too long.

While I had momentarily envisioned her coming to a halt just in front of me like my other horses often did when they came to greet me, she instead flew past me, throwing out a vicious kick as she went. It was aimed straight at my head.

A split second and a shift in trajectory spared me from a blow that could have been fatal. Instead, her hoof connected squarely with my right side. Pain exploded through my ribs, but I didn't cry out. I just gasped for breath, and let's be honest, threw an apple after her in vengeance while she galloped away, her nostrils flaring. It hurt me a lot more to throw the apple, than it hurt her to hear it go whizzing by, missing her entirely. I'm not proud of that moment, but for a second, I had held hope like a tiny flame in my heart, just for her damn freight train to run over it, snuffing it out entirely.

My side hurt for weeks afterward, but I didn't say a word to my mother until the bruising started to fade. How could I tell her that the horse we were trying so hard to help had tried to kill me? How could I tell her that her favorite was a lost cause? I couldn't. So, I bore the pain in silence, hoping against hope that the new treatment plan would bring about the change we so desperately needed. It eventually did, but by then, it was too late in some ways. Jazzy got better. Slowly, the fire in her eyes softened to a warm friendly glow, the tension in her jaw muscles eased and she stopped lashing out at everyone. We started to see glimpses of the horse underneath. But the damage was done. There was too much bad blood between her and most of the family. The fear and distrust that had built up during her illness lingered long after she recovered. It wasn't her fault, and it wasn't ours, but that didn't change the reality of existing together.

In the end, we made the hard decision, and we traded Jazz for a different horse. We hoped it would be a fresh start for all of us. And it was. We received so many photos of Jazz being ridden by her new owner and the owner's son, being pampered, being loved. We are to this day grateful for those owners, the vets who assisted along the way, and the buyers we purchased her from who were honest about her from the start. But sometimes, late at night, I wonder what would have happened if we'd known about the ulcers from the start. Would we have kept her?

Would the fear have never taken root? We'll never know. There are a lot of lessons I learned, and many should learn from Jazzy's tale. Don't judge something (or someone) by their outward appearance. How many of us have carried the weight of others' perceptions? It's never a pleasant feeling to be judged before you are known; and doing so to others can have catastrophic results. Never assume you have eliminated pain from the possible reasons for a behavior. 'We have ruled out pain' is not a valid statement when you cannot speak the same language as the one you have claimed to rule it out for.

Keep looking for the reason, keep up the good search for truth.

{Chapter 7}

If the shoe fits - Bud

Buds story is one in which the first part of his life is still a mystery. When we encountered him for the first time, he was already about eleven years old. A friend of my mother's had learned about him, and we went to see him. I know, that's lacking details but strangely enough neither my mother nor I could remember the exact scenario.

What we do remember in detail is seeing him for the first time. We pulled up to the tidy farm, admiring the manicured fence lines, neatly groomed flower beds, and the pristine white gravel drive. It was the kind of place that exuded an air of care and organization. We made our way past the house and into the farmyard to a small, unassuming metal machine shed at the edge of the property—nothing out of place, just a standard, mid-sized structure. When we were shown inside, however, it felt like stepping into a different world altogether. The door creaked open, and the first thing that struck us was how dark it was—so dark, in fact, that it took a few seconds for our eyes to adjust to the blackness. The only source of light came from a single bare bulb hanging from the ceiling, casting weak, pale shadows on the walls and floor. The second thing that hit us was the smell. It was suffocating. The ammonia-heavy stench of rank urine and compacted manure filled the small space, clawing at our throats and burning our eyes. It was like inhaling the very air of misery and neglect, so strong that it felt almost tangible. With the dim light from the bulb, we could just barely make out the shed's interior. It had been crudely divided into two sections by round pen panels—rusted and crusted with grime—and there were two stall doors on the right side of this sectioned-off area. The floor wasn't even visible under the thick layer of wet muck and manure that

coated it, deep and treacherous. A door along the far wall, which would have allowed fresh air into the space or let animals outside to escape the filth, was firmly shut, locking everything—every breath, every ounce of suffering—inside.

We made our way carefully across the muck-caked floor, our boots sticking with every step as if the place itself were trying to pull us down. There was a small, haphazardly shoveled-out area in front of one of the stall doors, just enough to allow the door to slide open slightly. The man, our guide through this horror, gestured to the stall and unlatched the door. With a heave, he pulled it open, the metal grinding painfully against its track. Inside, almost swallowed by the darkness, stood a horse. My heart sank as I took him in—knee-deep in filth, his legs lost in the muck and waste that had piled up over who knows how many months. The poor creature looked like he had been abandoned to rot, left to suffer in silence in this miserable, suffocating space. The ammonia had burned through his coat on his legs in spots exposing his skin. How things had gotten to this point, we never asked. It became a rescue mission and asking questions can sometimes make people defensive. There was no need for questions that may result in us not having access to the horse to help. The only thing that mattered was getting him out. Getting him somewhere—anywhere—that was clean, dry, and free of the darkness that had enveloped him. That day, without any trial or second thought, my mother purchased Bud, the poor, mistreated gelding who had been "advertised" as a kids' horse.

We didn't know what to expect once he was freed from his prison, and honestly, it didn't matter. Seeing him standing there, she knew that even if he was never rideable again, it was our duty to get him out of there and give him a chance at something better. Bud hobbled out of the stall slowly, his feet struggling to find purchase in the unstable muck.

Despite his condition—his skin marred by ammonia burns, his feet showing signs of neglect and possibly worse—he walked with a quiet dignity towards the trailer, he seemed to know that something was changing, that this was the beginning of something different. He cast one glance back at the shed as if to say goodbye to the darkness before stepping, cautiously but willingly, into the trailer.

Once home, we led him to an open, dry lot and a shelter with clean bedding, and let him rest. As Bud stood there, blinking in the sunlight, we could see his spirit lifting, his head coming up a little higher as he took in the clean air and space around him. The days that followed were filled with hope, but also with heartbreak. He tried, so hard, to run around his new pen—tried to feel what it was like to move freely again. But every time he attempted to canter, his legs would betray him, and he would stumble, falling into a crippling limp that sent him hobbling back to a walk. It was clear that whatever damage had been done was deep, and it would take time, if it ever healed at all.

Bud was an appaloosa horse, standing at around fifteen-two hands with a thick, foundational built frame, though you wouldn't have known it then with how gaunt he looked. His coat was a roaned-out grey, and while appaloosas are typically my favorite, Bud's coloring had a certain roughness to it—mottling around his nose and eyes that gave him a somewhat ghostly appearance. He wasn't the most attractive horse, I must admit, but he was a fighter, a horse that had been through hell but still had a gentleness about him, a willingness to trust, to try. When the farrier arrived so did the vet. Working with a care team is of major importance when rehabbing trauma and physical damage. Bud was a patient saint as we soon found out. He stood patiently until something hurt as they checked him over. As the farrier began trimming our horror only grew. Small clippers were used to start removing overgrown hoof which had turned slightly under.

His feet were full of scarred sole, and to our absolute dread, those large ridges we were observing on the front hooves – were horseshoe which had been grown over by hoof which then turned under. Two of his feet had encapsulated horseshoes.

Through a great deal of vet and farrier cooperation and guidance, the hooves were trimmed down, the shoes removed. He was even more sore initially following the removal of the shoes, they had been deep and the process of trimming them out had forced some decisions to trim into some less-than-ideal depths on the hoof wall. But healing is not linier, and it's not always pretty. Sometimes you take a step 'back' to go forward. Removing certain parts of the hoof in order to remove the foreign objects was part of that task for Buds care team.

For a couple months following the procedure, we familiarized ourselves with a crash course schedule of poultices, soaking, antibiotics, anti-inflammatory, and checkups. With time he made progress as the hooves grew out, and more of the damaged tissue was able to be trimmed away, leaving new healed tissue in its wake. In an unbelievable stroke of luck, none of the fine bone structure within the hooves had been damaged.

Bud was an amazing horse, patient, kind, steady.

But at the end of the day, he had one major flaw. He was unendingly vicious to Rocket. Rocket, having been my first horse ever, took priority to stay. So it was that Bud went to live with the friend of my mother's who had originally partnered with us to get him out of his situation. Ironically, upon arrival he was treated the same by her bay gelding as he had treated Rocket and Bud was so terrified of the tiny rotund mustang that he went through a couple of fences to get away from him.

Ultimately it was not a match either. The goal for Bud was always to find him the right home, not to keep him. But he had just turned out to be such a cool horse we each gave him a try as a keeper.

When the first prospective buyer came to see Bud, nearly eight months after we had rescued him from that dim, forsaken shed, we felt a cautious sense of optimism. It had been a long road of recovery for Bud—physically and mentally. He had gone from a horse with dull eyes and a gaunt frame to a vibrant, healthy gelding who though solidly lacking in distinct personality, was steady with meeting the world again. The countless hours grooming, caring for his feet, and letting him know he was safe had paid off. Bud's sound feet had returned, and with them, our hope that he could find a family who would cherish him.

The couple who came to see him that day were in their fifties, the kind of seasoned horse owners who enjoy their quiet time on the trails and know a good horse when they see one. They lived near a state park known for its winding trails, scenic overlooks, and quiet glades—an ideal spot for trail riding. As we made small talk, they spoke fondly of the peaceful rides they took together, just enjoying the rhythm of hoofbeats on a dirt path, away from the noise and stress of daily life. It sounded like the perfect place for Bud, who had proven himself a gentle and calm trail horse in the time we'd had him.

When we're assessing potential buyers, there's a lot more that goes into the decision than just financial considerations. We look at everything—how the rider approaches the horse, their confidence level, the respect they show when they ask to handle him. You'd be surprised how many people reveal their true colors in these moments, showing impatience or roughness when they think no one's watching. I could tell you stories about buyers who seemed pleasant and considerate in conversation, only to yank on a horse's mouth or kick too hard when they get a little distance away and think you cannot see. For us, a horse's happiness and well-being always come first, so we vet our buyers carefully.

That's why, as the man began interacting with Bud, we watched him closely. He spoke softly and moved slowly, giving Bud time to get used to his presence.

He ran his hands along Bud's muscles and checked his feet for rocks and gave a nod of approval when Bud responded calmly. (We disclosed fully his previous hoof situation) It was clear they were kind-hearted, with a genuine interest in Bud's comfort and needs.

We had priced Bud modestly, under the label of a "walks nicely down a trail, not a show horse but solid and safe" kind of price. He wasn't the fanciest horse in our barn, but he had a gentle demeanor that made him perfect for leisurely rides. We figured he'd be ideal for a couple like this, who just wanted a companion to enjoy the beauty of nature with. What happened next took us by complete surprise.

The man mounted Bud with ease, adjusting his reins and shifting his weight naturally, as though they had been partners for years. Instead of heading straight down the little path like we expected, he asked Bud to perform a series of maneuvers that caught us completely off-guard. With a slight nudge and an almost imperceptible cue, Bud moved through a complex series of lateral movements— leg yields, shoulder-ins, and collected trot transitions that were executed flawlessly. Our jaws practically hit the ground. We'd had Bud for months and had never once thought to ask him for anything beyond horsy kindergarten basic commands. He had always been cooperative, but these advanced skills suggested a much higher level of training than we'd ever imagined. Bud wasn't just a trail horse; he was educated, responsive, and capable of movements that pointed to a background in a completely different discipline. Had he been a dressage horse once? A ranch horse with years of experience? We had no way of knowing, but watching him that day, it was clear Bud had a history we hadn't uncovered.

The couple was equally stunned, exchanging glances that spoke volumes.

"Seems like he's got a few more tricks up his

sleeve," the husband remarked, smiling broadly as Bud came to a halt with the gentlest of touches. He dismounted, and I could see it on their faces—the decision had already been made. They had come looking for a quiet, uncomplicated trail partner, but they had found something much more—a horse with the kind of training and responsiveness that's hard to come by. They were thrilled, even if they didn't plan to put Bud's advanced skills to use every day. It was a bonus, a hidden gem they hadn't expected.

As they spoke about their home, their property near the park, and their intention to make Bud a part of their family, we knew it was the right match. They weren't buying Bud for what he could do for them; they were choosing him for who he was, a horse who had been through hardship and come out the other side stronger and more resilient. They promised to give him the peaceful life he deserved—long trail rides, a roomy paddock, and plenty of love.

When Bud stepped onto their trailer that afternoon, there was no hesitation, no looking back. He was ready, as if he knew that his next chapter was going to be a good one. It's a rare and beautiful thing when you find the perfect match for a horse you've poured your heart into, and this felt like one of those moments.

Bud went on to live out the rest of his days with that wonderful family, spending his time exploring the trails he was made for, with people who adored him. They sent us pictures and updates often—Bud standing by the lakeside with the wife, Bud plodding along a sun-dappled path with the husband happily aboard, Bud with what little mane he had braided by their granddaughter who had taken a special shine to him and occasionally rode him on the trails too.

We never found out what had caused Bud to end up in that dark shed. Was he once a show horse? A family companion? Whatever his past, it had been lost in the shadows of that place, buried under layers of filth and neglect and replaced with shining rays of love and belonging.

I thought a long while about including Buds story in this book. At first, I wasn't sure what the message was that was original to his story. Then as I went back over the details, I realized there didn't need to be one. Bud wasn't the first horse to teach me to rescue, or the first one to win my heart. He wasn't the flashiest, or the closest to death's door when we took him on. His story simply left me reconfirming that you don't have to be the most spectacular

to be important and special. The world loves a good show, lots of flash, and the prettiest of everything. We prioritize and place on a pedestal those who achieve, and glow; but everyone is special, every horse is special, and that's enough all on its own. He wasn't the 'most' anything, but he was so much all on his own.

{Chapter 8}

A Product of His Sport - Buck

You remember Buck, right? He's that "barrel horse" I traded Cicero for. You'll notice those quotation marks around barrel horse, and I'll tell you all about it. There are more stories than I could possibly fit in this book about Buck, and by the end of it, you may think I am certifiably crazy but that's a chance I'll just have to take. The ad I found for Buck had maybe four sentences. It was listed on some backwater message board in the earlier days of the internet where horses were listed for sale; and while I don't remember the exact ad, I remember it didn't even have a picture.

You'll hear me say this a lot in relation to Buck and our journey. I have no idea who in their right mind inquires on an ad like that. But I did.

It rained. The freezing rain you shouldn't be driving in and certainly shouldn't be out looking at a horse in, but we had driven quite a way to do this viewing, and the sellers were meeting us at the barn. We arrived and found out that - luck us - the driveway was flooded, and no car could go up. Holding on tight to the warmth left over from the car, we walked roughly eighth mile up through the torrent of weather. Oh, and better yet, there was only an outdoor arena. We huddled into the tiny barn which had standing only slots for each horse. Attempting to keep our teeth from chattering out of our heads while she tightened up the girth and led him out. I viewed this 'speed demon' barrel horse. He was plain. His coat shown mostly white apart from large brown spots on his chest, flank, and head.

He was a bit thin on the topline even with the saddle covering his back. He had a scar on his face from an old fence injury which had created a sort of nub of scar tissue the size of a small grape sticking out midway down his blaze. One eye was blue, the other brown, and his nose was a soft pink. I hoped he had patience with us as we asked him to work some in this despicable cold.

He spooked coming out of the barn, spooked at a car parked behind the barn, spooked at a tarp on an upright cart alongside the barn, and again at the puddles in the driveway while walking across to the arena. That was...promising. The arena was a mess of slop, the view between the downpouring rain and the steam coming up from my own breath made seeing much of anything difficult. The wind stung as it pelted ice chips into our faces and we made our way out. I have no idea who in their right mind goes to see a horse in that weather. But I did; and I was rewarded with the most magnificent creature I have seen to this day.

The girl riding him clearly didn't know the barrel racing pattern. She consistently took him backwards around the barrels. I'm not talking went left instead of the usual right as some riders prefer but went in front, then looped around back. He was also clearly aggravated at the lack of speed which was necessary with the ground conditions. At this point we were happy to be able to see him move at all, but running was not a good idea.

Buck was frustrated, over-bitted, and under impressed with our idea of a good time. He grunted, snorted, and threw his head most of the ride for her but, he never offered to protest in a more outspoken manner, and she neared the end of the ride without incident despite clearly being scared of his behavior. While he was on the majority of the ride, I was only marginally interested in him. He moved nicely if you could see it past the head tossing, which I didn't blame him for in the conditions. But the last lap she brought him around at a trot along the rail.

As they turned the far corner and came in line with me just inside the fence down the long side of the arena, I really saw Buck.

As a teenager, you're not always looking for the logical choice. Sometimes it's a moment meant to be for entirely different reasons than logic. Here was Buck; his head was high, his nostrils flared like some sort of wild dragon complete with steam thanks to the weather. The wide chest and high action legs paired with the flowing movement of his entire body as it cut through the sheet of rain brandishing the shield marking on his chest as if charging into battle. Here was a horse I could conquer my world on. Here was the magic I had been looking for. I didn't need to see the whole ride I had seen up to that point, I didn't need to ride him myself, I could have seen just that one stretch of arena, and I was his.

We arranged for them to see our mare Cicero a couple weeks later closer to our home and thank goodness in calmer weather and they brought Buck with. We arrived at our meeting location early, a friend's house with an indoor arena. When they arrived with Buck we were in shock. I thought they had brought us the wrong horse. Out from the trailer stepped the fattest bellied horse I had ever seen. I figured they grabbed the wrong horse from the pasture, someone else must have loaded it for them because this was surely a heavily pregnant mare, not the gelding I had seen a mere few weeks ago! The barn had a concrete aisle which ran along the long side of the indoor arena in front of the barn's multiple stalls. It was necessary to bring the horses through on that path to get to the arena gate inside. But they could not get him in the door as he was snorting and shaking so hard his legs were near collapse. I feel terrible about it now, but I'll admit, my mother and I laughed under our breath. It may not have been the best reaction at the time but holy horse I have never seen knees buckle so badly that an enormous belly nearly scraped the ground as he still attempted to walk! It was quite a sight and pretty well evaporated any impression of coolness I had seen in this horse the first viewing on his home turf. It took nearly half an hour to get him to the arena gate and inside. Once on the sand he was much relieved and went about his business while I showed them Cicero being ridden.

My mother – having eyes, and a brain and all – had questions for me about my certainty in this gelding for obvious reasons. I was trading a calm cool collected younger papered mare for something slightly older, unpapered, and clearly a little off anxiety wise. Not to mention I hadn't ridden him yet. But we fixed that last part when I told her I was certain, and I jumped on that day.

He was fiery, like a sports car when I had been working with reliable sedans most of my life. He crowhopped for seemingly no reason, he ran hard, turned hard, and grunted and grumbled the whole time even if I asked gently. He was a reactive animal with very little 'thinking brain' and I was in love. I have no idea who in their right mind gets on a horse like that. But I did.

Chalk it up to teenage stupid bravery but he was mine. I have no idea who in their right mind buys a horse like that. But I did...Then I tried to sell him for almost two years.

Yes, you read it right. We didn't click, he was a lot. I mean a whole lot of horse. He couldn't run the barrels without trying to jump on top of them instead of going around. His cues were out of a different dictionary than any riding language I had ever learned, and he literally spooked at his own shadow – frequently. Buck didn't lunge, didn't stand tied, didn't like grooming apart from bath time. The little Tovero gelding untied himself from the trailer and took off frequently while I was tacking up.

He tried to throw me every time my emotions were even slightly less than perfectly level – try working with that as a teenage girl whose parents are going through a divorce. He was figuratively and literally hardheaded and would routinely throw his head bringing his rock-hard jawbone down on my skull on the way over top of me. I had split lips, headaches, a hurt nose and a lot of hurt ego moments in those early days.

We had potential buyers. Some were too rough on him, and I declined to sell a horse to them. Others were perfect and told us he was perfect, then never followed up to purchase for whatever reason. I was offered trades on occasion, but most where the other horse was obviously lame, or mis advertised, which I turned down of course.

Nothing ever worked out for my plan to sell this horse. Despite price decreases, listing him everywhere and doing my best to improve his training while I still had him fate did not want us apart!

The day came when I knew I was missing something. I had already had his back, his feet, his teeth and his nutrition checked. He had been seen by everyone who could have an educated opinion apart from a trainer who at the time we couldn't afford as an extra expense. So, the proverb became true for us "Necessity is the mother of invention" or the mother of discovery in this case.

Buck was the first horse I ever 'deconstructed' and rebuilt an entire knowledge set on. To this day when I am training I choose to call it 'installing the thinking brain'. To create an animal who thinks before reacting. One who trusts and has been trained away from their reactive prey mentality. We found a natural horsemanship trainer whose methods seemed to click, I bought the videos, we moved forward on a new and upward path as partners.

I had this blossoming relationship with Buck through many dark years of my life. We helped each other learn and grow. When high school came, I designed my class ring to look like his crystal blue eye. I found my religion upon his back in my late teen years and I am eternally thankful to him for giving me the sense of quiet in myself while I tried to figure him out. It directly resulted in me finding myself. Buck met me in my chaos, with a chaos all his own to match it, and we clawed and pulled each other out. Sometimes the most unexpected gifts lie in our greatest challenges.

It is with the proudest, and fullest heart I share that my heart horse is still with me in our growing eighteen years of partnership. His back sags some, his steps are shorter and slower at twenty-eight and lord knows he's missing all but three teeth, none of which align to the others; but as I feed him warmed mash, pet his seemingly self-cleaning white coat, and sit in the quiet we have built for each other he is still everything I ever wanted. He is everything I never knew I needed.

I have no idea who is so lucky to own a horse like that. But I do.

{Chapter 9}

I need a Hero – Hero

I've taken on a few contracts in my day for training horses private party. None quite so large as a long winter contract to train as many horses as possible for a spring sale. The barn owner would purchase horses as he saw fit, and had a couple lined up already at the barn. While I'm no stranger to an assortment of ailments, lameness issues, and character quirks, I learned more that winter than ever before.

The owner was an aged gentleman who believed very much in the old training methods. Natural horsemanship or, in my opinion, even common-sense horsemanship was not his forte. In addition, he believed that a horse must be high-headed, and prancing, to be impressive; that is the only reason someone will buy a horse. At the onset of our agreement, we discussed my leanings towards natural horsemanship and the fact that I refuse to rush a horse into a situation since it most often ends poorly. Do more on the ground first, and you'll get a better first ride and long-term relationship than if you just jump on.

It was agreed upon that I would do my job, my way, and he would in turn 'stay out of my way' – his words not mine. It was unfortunate then that along our partnership journey, this was not honored in a number of ways. We continued to find differences in opinion on how the horses should be treated and trained. Some things were smaller than others but still lacked the commonsense aspect I was attempting to put into all training for my own safety and the safety of the horse and its future buyers.

Things like the fact that a horse we were planning to market for children and as child safe, should be able to walk, not just bolt around with a rider. Or that carrying a flag was clearly the most important way to attract rodeo queens to purchase the horses when groundwork and desensitization the things which would allow a horse to function to even attend an event where he may carry the flag had been skipped. You know, small things.

The first day Hero came to the barn, I arrived to train as usual, pulling up on the crunching gravel drive to the big brown barn I was excited to see the newest project. I had been informed that he had "some soreness". The horse with no name was being kept in a pen outside of the main barn. It was midwinter, and the sun sat early, so the path outside the barn was dark other than a small semicircle illuminated by the aisle lights. Upon watching the gelding attempt to walk into the barn from the small outdoor pen I at first thought the shadows and light were deceiving my eyes. I suffer from a case of night blindness which certainly distorts how I see in some situations where the light is glaring, and complete darkness is nearby. How I wish this had been one of those times. The tall dull coated sorrel gelding, with the slightly enlarged knees, and tracking his hind end distinctly out of line with his front end tried his best to walk with the barn handler from his pen. It was a snail's pace, a three-legged lame shuffle-hop. What was worse, he was in so much visible full-body pain with large sections of muscle tying up, but he attempted to move for the man anyways. Some soreness didn't even begin to cover it. He was a fairly young horse, maybe six or seven years old. His sixteenhand plus frame was covered in a mealy sorrel brown coat. He had tall thin ears, a drawn face, and too little meat on his bones, but not quite emaciated.

One of the major items myself and my employer disagreed on was the use of a veterinarian for anything other than last moment euthanasia. Where I saw a need to immediately have this animal seen and start getting vital information about what was happening in his body, we could not resolve our differences when he refused to see anything but loss of profits.

Because of this difference of opinion, I worked with what I had available to me to do everything I could for the gelding while not being a vet. My initial hope was that we could resolve this and move forward. We agreed on a feeding regimen and the horse was being well kept basic needs wise from a feed, water, and shelter point of view. I had seen the photos of where he came from and quite frankly, the situation he was currently in was a big step up. So, I devised a plan to make him as comfortable as I could. I remember many a night those first few weeks in his stall with a bucket of steaming warm water infused with liniment. The near meditative smell of eucalyptus and the warm peace of healing in the air. Most nights I spent sponging him down and massaging, sending up prayers with the tendrils of steam into the rafters and hoping that some of his pain would be resolved. He so often turned his head to me with big, ever softening eyes and nuzzled my arm as if to say thank you.

Three weeks in, Hero (the name I settled on for him after hearing it from a dear co-worker of mine) and I were in the arena working on some basic directed free movement. He was allowed to go anywhere in the big arena he wanted, I just wanted him to periodically change directions and to keep moving at whatever pace was comfortable. So often, movement breaks up restriction in muscles and it was my hope to see if he would benefit from the movement, or if I could narrow down if he had a muscle disorder. It was a quiet day in the barn, just me and the horses. Hero was brave, and growing stronger every day despite still limping, and sometimes wobbling just a bit when he tried to move faster than a walk. It was a vast improvement from where we started. This day was special.

As he moved around, I asked that he change directions, and he voluntarily took a little half jump and started trying to play with me. I was elated. His small moment brought tears to my eyes. Who knows how long it had been since he felt like playing. Since he had opened up to a human being and said, 'here is my personality, I want to meet you'. I was so happy his joy showed even past his pain, even if it was only for a moment. It was a sign that his body felt good enough to try for the first time, and he was safe and connected enough with me to play. The moment was unceremoniously shattered when we heard from the other side of the arena "good, it looks like it's about time to put a saddle on him and get started" I hadn't even seen the barn owner come in. Somewhere lost in the heights of my joy and awe, at first, I thought it was a joke. I remember responding with lighthearted sarcasm along the lines of "oh yeah, he doesn't have a long way to go or anything." As it turned out he wasn't joking.

I attempted to reason with the owner including a good amount of downright pleading to let a vet take a look at Hero. I offered to pay for the initial vet appointment, and told him if the vet came, and indicated there shouldn't have been an appointment because nothing was wrong with Hero then he would take no loss of profits. Theres no risk when you know you're right, so bet all the chips needed.

My plea was declined.

Hero was not my only project. Two of the other horses I was overseeing were being pushed too fast as well. While trying to hurry one along to the speed I was now being pushed for, the owner made some poor decisions and startled the other gelding badly while I was aboard. It ended up getting me launched into a telephone pole. I wore the pain of that incident in my back and shoulders for years to come.

A week later, after several more pushes to appeal the decision on a vet appointment I quit the contract and all its horses. I was being pushed to get on Hero and my morals would not permit me to do this to an animal and push it past its clear physical limits.

I went back to my routines with my own horses and tried to forget. But thoughts of the horses I had left at the training barn persisted. They were fed, cared for in the most basic required ways, and I hoped anyone else who was hired would tell him the same things I had. Perhaps if many said the same, he would see his unrealistic expectations for what they were.

Later online I saw the horses had been handed to another trainer. Younger and newer than myself. They were being marketed in all sorts of inaccurate ways, but exactly how I had been pushed to do so. Their incorrect ages and heights were the least worrying things in the ads.

In fact, they were being marketed as a finished version of what we had planned though there had not been adequate time to accomplish that goal. They were nowhere near the horses that were being advertised. And while Hero was never marketed and from what I heard from barn goers remained retired to a pasture. I hope though for the others and their owners that it worked out somehow.

Hero is one of the horses I must thank for setting me on a path to bodywork, to kinesiology taping, to doing better for our equine friends and their strong but simultaneously delicate and complicated bodies. I speculate, looking back with my now broader knowledge base that Hero was the unfortunate embodiment of a disorder called Polysaccharide Storage Myopathy (PSSM for short) which can cause similar symptoms to what he was displaying, or HYPP which is a genetic disorder within the Quarter Horse world with somewhat overlapping symptoms. I was honored to have been a person with which this gentle soul shared his playful personality, and through which he had some peace, even just for a moment. Hero taught me through his strength and resilience that courage isn't always a grand spectacle, sometimes it is the bravery to just keep trying.

It is my understanding that he has gone to the pasture in the sky where I am sure he is running with great joy and no more pain.

{Chapter 10}

Not a Chance – Mina

Life happens. It is inevitable and honestly, we have all been there. Been in a situation where life caused us to have to sell and rehome things or animals we loved. I have been there personally, forced to make tough decisions for animals who were part of a business, part of my family and who I had promised would be with me forever. It is heartbreaking but sometimes totally unavoidable. This story comes from a situation of that type and the owners did the best they could for their horses.

My mother wanted a baby. No, not that kind of baby, she already had me and I think I have given her enough grey hair for a lifetime, she couldn't survive another one of us after myself and my two daredevil brothers. A foal was on her wish list though. At that time, I was also looking for a project to train and re-sell. So, when my ad was answered we found ourselves going to see a barrel racing bred bay mare and her young palomino foal in the deepest of winter.

We arrived to see the two horses standing on the front lawn with a bale of rich alfalfa, the bright green in contrast to the barren brown and white of the winter surrounding them. The filly was young, born out of normal foaling season and not yet weaned. It was difficult to get a good look at her as she hid on whichever side of her mother was opposite from us. She was cute and in the right age range. The mare left much to be desired in temperament and build but would have done well with weight gain, and a workout plan.

Neither of us was totally sold on the pair as what we had been looking for. The property had lots of other horses in various pens, and with the owner sharing the fact that they all needed to be sold, we asked if we could look around and were granted that privilege. In the front pen, my mother found a young filly and her dam which were incredibly promising. The mare was already sold and had a new home coming to get her soon but the grey filly (now affectionately known as Storm with us) was the first to join our purchase list. As we wandered to the biggest pasture on the property, a loud black and white paint mare came into my view, along with a white pony (who you will read about in another chapter of this book). A number of horses were in the space eating straw round bales. Suddenly the bay mare out front and her aggressive attitude made sense. She was protecting the alfalfa. It must have been hard to nurse a foal on nutritionally deficient straw, her body had certainly shown it.

The black and white mare was in good shape apart from needing her hooves addressed badly. She and another dun pinto mare stood close to each other like best friends and allowed me to look over them both. Secret time – I typically don't care for black and white pintos – but something in this mares eyes was stunning. It's like seeing a soul that's been around a few times vs ones that's new to this earth if you'll allow me the reincarnation reference.

There are some animals who simply have more depth of personality and spirit than others, and this mare had oceans of it pooled within her beautiful eyes. I leaned close to her and felt tears start to well up from nowhere.

We had worked with and purchased quite a few horses in my life, but this one spoke so loud in her quiet that it touched my soul and sent little pieces of it sliding down my cheeks.

"We're going to bring you home and we are going to love you" I promised her. Mina as we started calling her almost immediately, became the second horse on the purchase list. One of the most heart wrenching things I have had to do, since we hadn't brought a trailer, was to say that to this animal, and then walk away. She didn't know it was just for a day or two until we could come back. As she saw us retreat from the pen she became bothered, as if she thought I was breaking my promise already. She moved to the gates, urgent in her attempt to regain our attention. It killed us to have to leave her even for that day.

After what turned out to be two weeks later due to icy Midwest conditions, Mina, Storm, and a white pony (now called Ollie) from the farm were delivered to us. They all looked fantastic, and I was glad they were home.

In fact, Mina looked quite – rotund. I inquired on whether she could be pregnant. I was assured it was the new round bales, it was a hay belly. Having seen a great many hay bellies, I was somewhat skeptical. The bulge sure looked low and far back to be a hay belly growing there on my new mare.

Weeks went by and we worked with the new horses on various skills and began weaving them slowly into our existing herd following a thirty-day quarantine. The weather was cold and abysmal that winter, including a polar vortex which found us getting downright creative fitting nine stalls into a thirty by fifty foot shed rather than relying on the outdoor lean to shelters.

As daily care and enrichment, we groomed and spent extended time with each horse in those all-indoor days. It was during that time we noticed something odd. I was spending some time with Mina in her makeshift stall; grooming and petting. She wasn't a huge fan of being touched any further back than her shoulders when she first arrived. We had worked on her skills picking up her feet and being able to groom more areas of her body. She was coming along nicely. As my brush passed over her underbelly, a bulge pushed out from her side, then went back to the soft rounded surface it had been a moment before. I rubbed my eyes, surely that was just her adjusting and her flank flexing. I didn't see it again inthat session and honestly chalked it up to some strange muscle flexes. I had never had a pregnant mare; I wasn't sure what that looked like, but I had seen my other horses' sides expand out to a much lesser degree then flatten again on occasion.

The next day my mother and I were standing outside of Minas stall, once again stall hopping with grooming kits and all the cuddles for the horses. When an undeniable bulge popped out again, then went back in. I remember looking to mom and saying "Well, either it's an alien or someone was wrong about if she was in with a stallion at any point"

I ordered an equine pregnancy test online that night and eagerly awaited the mail. I would have bribed the mailman with just about anything if I could have made it arrive faster. I felt the need to know definitively even having seen proof. The urine test promised to be able to show which trimester the mare was in. I also reached out to the previous owners again. Turns out my Mina and their mares in the herd had spent just a couple of days in with a very young stallion. They were not even certain he could produce yet. I informed them without doubt, that he produced just fine.

I spent the next several months – let's be honest – annoying Mina until she loved me. Annoying her to let me touch not only past her shoulders, but now in my urgency before a foal arrived; to be able to touch even the most intimate places on her body in the event something went wrong with the upcoming birth. She was placed on the vets recommended diet, and thoroughly checked over once they could get her appointment scheduled.

As for me, I spent the next couple of months reading everything I could get my hands on. Online articles, books, blogs, magazines, and lots of coat color predictors. That smokey black grulla tobiano sure sounded good! Better yet if I could get my favorite markings on the face and legs. But the chances were so slim at six percent. Any color would be fine I decided. I had never had a foal born from one of our horses, and you would have thought I was the one having the baby! In possibly the most outrageous claim ever I even turned down going to a bachelorette party over a month in advance with the reason "I just know it's going to be that Saturday." I didn't know, or at least I didn't know that I knew; but I had a gut feeling.

Call me the midwife of horses because on that Saturday over a month later, Mina's water broke, and the filly began her introduction to the wide world from her mother's womb. The first of her sires foals and the first of my Minas.

Once Minas water broke, I read we had about thirty minutes before the delivery. I stepped out of the shed where the phone reception was hopeless and attempted to call the neighbors to see if they wanted to come watch the birth. I no sooner heard the first ring on the phone line when my mother yelled "You had better get back in here! It's coming now!" Surely as the sun rises, tall white socks emerged above the tiny front hooves protruding into the world, followed by a delicate head with a narrow-centered white strip. Our marvelous Mina completed the whole initial event in approximately ten minutes. The filly – taking after her mother – came out guns a blazing. Foals, as we understood it, normally stayed fairly still through birth and for a bit of time after. It's nature's way of letting nutrients transfer from mother to young through the umbilical cord, and a way of keeping the foal from kicking while the hind legs are still within the mare. Not Minas little one, she came out kicking and we removed her hind legs from Mina so she would not cause injury.

Large bold spots adorned her whole body in black and white, a carbon copy of her mother's dazzling color. We named the foal Melody and watched in amazement and a flood of happy tears as Mina learned how to be a mother for the first time.

Both Mina and her filly are still with me today and bring me a great deal of joy. Melody took some inspiration from both parents and upon losing her foal coat came out to be the smokey black grulla tobiano, with four tall white socks, there was less

than six percent outcome – What was the chance? –
Couldn't have designed her or her mother better
myself.

{Chapter 11}

Quite a trip – Angel

There are some downright dishonest people in the world—no question about it. And nowhere are lies more dangerous than in the horse world, where misinformation can put both people and horses at serious risk. A thousand plus pound animal, misrepresented in its abilities or temperament, can easily cause harm if not accurately described. But when your passion for horses runs as deep, you take those risks in stride, believing in the good of people until proven otherwise.

I had always been fascinated by the art of equine stunt riding, otherwise known as trick riding. It's an adrenaline-fueled discipline where riders perform death defying stunts on horseback : vaulting, hanging from stirrups, and balancing in ways that make spectators gasp. I was captivated from the very first moment I saw it.

Determined to be part of this craft, I sought out the best trainer I could find and dove into the world of trick riding, embracing every fall, bruise, and ache that came with it. I had never felt more alive. Trick riders are a different breed—relentless, resilient, and tougher than nails. My mother thought she had finally had one child who was not a daredevil. My brothers loved stunt riding motorcycles for kicks, and taking offroad vehicles up the sides of mountains and glaciers for goodness sakes, maybe one kid could not give her heart attacks. Then I informed her of this new adventure I was undertaking – Sorry mom.

When the time finally came for me to purchase my own trick horse, I wanted a partner who could keep me safe as I pushed my limits. I found what seemed like the perfect match—a stunning palomino draft cross mare named Angel, with a flowing mane and tail that looked straight out of a shampoo commercial. The sellers assured me she had been used for trick riding before. Horses with this kind of training and beauty don't stay on the market long, so I wasted no time in scheduling a visit to see her.

The barn was small, and the owners were eager to show her off. I explained my specific need for a trick horse and asked to see her perform. The tricks they showed were minor and a bit half-hearted, but I chalked it up to the limitations of their small indoor arena. It felt right, especially since we all shared the same trainer. I trusted them and took their words as truth. When I asked why they were selling her, I was told it was because they needed another Roman riding horse of similar size to the one they currently owned. For those unfamiliar, Roman riding is a breathtaking act where the rider stands with one foot on each of two horses as they move in unison, side by side. It's a discipline that requires two matched horses (at least height wise), and since Angel didn't fit that bill, she was up for sale. I was thrilled—everything seemed to align perfectly. I had found my dream horse, one who could help me navigate the daring sport I grew to love more every day.

The day of delivery arrived, and our golden mare stepped off the trailer looking every bit as beautiful as I remembered. But as the hauler closed the trailer door and prepared to leave, the driver leaned out of the truck window, tossing out a few last words:

"Oh, by the way, please don't trick ride her."

I stood there, stunned and confused, as they drove away. Don't trick ride her? But that was the entire reason I'd bought her! It was the skill set I'd inquired about and the very thing they had said she had done. I couldn't wrap my head around it. I called the sellers repeatedly, only to be met with radio silence. Something was very wrong.

With no answers, I reached out to my trainer, hoping for some clarification. "I got a horse," I said, trying to mask the anxiety tightening in my chest.

"Oh? Tell me about it," she responded warmly.

"She's a big, beautiful palomino. I bought her from another one of your students…"

There was a long pause before she spoke again.

"You didn't buy Angel, did you?"

"Yes… why?"

"That horse put her owner in the hospital."

My heart sank. My dream was unraveling before my eyes. All the money I had saved up, the hours of training, and the excitement of moving forward in my passion, it all came crashing down with those few words.

Angel had been misrepresented, and I had been sold a lie that had cost me more than just money—it shattered my hopes of continuing in the sport. This deception robbed me of the dream I had worked so hard to build, and to this day, it remains one of the few betrayals I have never quite forgiven.

Life has a way of surprising us though, even in the midst of disappointment. Despite everything, Angel turned out to be a true blessing in disguise. She had a subtle gait flaw that made it impossible for her to support a rider's weight hanging off her side while running as she would trip. The last place you want to be when a horse trips, is hanging from it in a vulnerable position. It explained why she was no longer fit for trick riding and why she should never have been advertised as such. Yet, she possessed an incredibly gentle and kind spirit. With proper vet care and management, she could be ridden as a normal horse would be, so long as she wasn't asked to jump or take on heavy work. She quickly became my mother's personal horse when we went riding and they looked just like twins walking down the road with their blonde ponytails swaying. Angel thrived in a different role as well, teaching young children how to ride and giving them the confidence to grow as equestrians.

Angel was, in every sense, an angel. Her soundness issues were manageable for years, and she became a cornerstone of my riding program, patiently guiding little ones who looked up at her massive frame with awe in their eyes. She formed connections that transformed lives, becoming the first horse many kids ever rode. In the end, she found her true purpose, one that seemed to bring her much happiness. As she aged, the old knee injury that had plagued her began to catch up, slowing her down. We kept her comfortable with joint medications, giving her the best care possible.

Years later when her body finally began to fail her, we retired her to our sunny pasture where she spent her last days peacefully grazing and basking in the warmth of the sun. We were fortunate to have her until the very end and grateful for the time she spent blessing our lives.

There are some downright dishonest people in the world, and Angel's story is a testament to that. But in a strange, unexpected way, she ended up being one of the best lies I was ever told. She may not have been the trick horse I had dreamed of, but she was a teacher, a healer, and a gentle soul who blessed our lives in more ways than I could have imagined. And that's a truth I will always cherish.

{Chapter 12}

Tag 1432 – Posey

The first time Posey and I met was a real wake up
call. Until that April I had never met a horse who
came from an actual kill pen. Horses that were being
sold to, shipped to, were originally bought from, or
promised to a kill pen yes, but not one who had so
recently endured the darkness of one of those
dreadful places. Deemed tag# 1432 he had been
shipped up from Texas after going through the pen,
then thirty days quarantine before being trailered
the roughly 1,100 miles, never getting out of the
trailer. Posey's owner had called me to come out and
quote training him to stop walking on her and stop
being so flinchy about everything. It wasn't a

surprise that a horse which had been through what he had was exhibiting bad habits. It was late April when I met him but he had been at the stable already since February.

Posey was purchased on a social media page through a kill pen rescue. Who knows why tag # 1432 –

"10 year old 14.2H – very gentle & broke to ride" – was there, or how long, but the group helping to rescue these horses typically only posts those about to be shipped out.

He had five days; his deadline was almost up. His owner mercifully rescued him through the group, funded his bail, his quarantine and his trailer trip north.

What I found was heartbreaking. It was not that I expected a show horse by any means; I have rescued

before and there isn't much pretty to behold on the front end of the process. But this possibly 14.1H on a good day, clearly younger than ten, battered little disheveled buckskin pony broke my heart as did the other details of just how much he didn't do. The owners had done so much already to try to improve him. His shaggy ratted mane had been cut off to start anew, they had tried to save it but to no avail. They had gotten a vet out to see him when he first arrived and given him a bath while he was still sedated that day as well as trimmed much needed length off his feet. It was the only way it could be accomplished. His eyes were tight and mistrusting, and thick black scars riddled the lower part of both his back legs, perhaps from a barb wire fence incident. A large surface gap ran down the back left hoof, looking very well like a rod of some sort had grown in then been pulled out. We later found out the cornet band had been so damaged that his hoof would never grow pretty again, it would always grow with that same gap. I simply thanked God he was still sound despite the cosmetics.

I knew he was a much bigger job than I had been called for after hearing the details about the vet visit, but that fact was solidified when I entered the stall with him. In the shade and shadow of the stall Posey plastered himself to the wooden wall in the back. He looked like he would do his best chameleon impression and blend right into the wood given the option. Since it was in fact not an option, he settled for dancing his feet around and stomping to show me he would indeed kill anything that came close. I was going to be that thing. With a good long pause, a small prayer, and just a pinch of stupidity, I walked through the door. I told God again and again, you guided me to this purpose, please don't let him be the one to suddenly communicate to me that you have changed your mind! My experience whispered in my head the phrases he's simply broken, he's broken; he can't cry like humans, he couldn't scream at the sky or talk to someone about it.

He was in the world of animals(us) which he now considered predators; all he could do was survive us. He snorted at me like a freight train lived inside his lungs, moving with painfully clear intent if I came closer. Maybe this one was too far gone. Maybe he was not advertised honestly, maybe he was entirely wild. Most horses I have experience with would have figured out I wasn't even moving by now and stopped prancing and panicking. Not Posey. He danced in place the whole time on the wall, threatening my fate based on my next move.

So, I didn't move forward, but I didn't retreat from his threats. Instead, I knelt, the very act of which spooked him more and he snorted his disapproval. I did not insist that he trust me or live with my rules. Rather I gave him my trust.

In the not so large stall, he could have kicked me in the face, tried to charge, or trampled me into dust along with the woodchips on the mats. I prayed as I watched him. Let me help this little horse. What has this creature been through? I waited and waited until my feet cramped from the position, then I waited more afraid to move and scare him again. My reward.... He looked at me.

That's right, he looked at me, not sized me up, not

feared, took a pause and looked. He ceased his stomping for a moment and a short wave of relaxation came through his eyes. They became more liquid than stone for the first time. His look was honest, pure, gentle, but it said so much.

"I can't" the look said

"But WE can" I told him.

The big moment that first day came when I was able to touch his shoulder. It came with a snort and a nip at me on his part, but it was progress. I knew the whole story had not been conveyed when from outside of the stall I heard a whisper from the woman to one of the barn crew.

"Oh my gosh she got to touch him" – So much for just being hired to fix a couple minor bad habits.

I initially took Posey on for thirty days beginning in June of that year. As it turned out he didn't really do anything as advertised. I'm not saying the company lied; In fact, I adore them for what they do for these animals. But the fact was when they said "ride-able" because he was paralyzed with fear so terribly that someone could sit on him for a photo. They didn't do the proper evaluation. You couldn't touch Posey past his shoulder until he was in such a panic that he completely mentally locked up. Had they asked him to take one step in that evaluation they quickly would have realized their error. I am proud to report that this company now does riding videos when they post horses.

In June we began our journey together in the warmth of the oncoming summer. My first session with him outside his stall and arena at their property made my initial impression of him not much better than the first in the stall.

I spent the better part of an hour getting a halter on him that first day in the paddock. The terror filled buckskin thought the whole world would kill him. The round pen gate took well over twenty min as well to get through at any speed less than a bolt. Convinced it would grab him he nearly ran me over the first roughly fifty times through.

We battled through a number of worldly – and imaginary monsters over the next few weeks. Stripes on the road were poisonous snakes to him; the trees were monsters grabbing in the wind. And me? I was still questionable at best.

My fiancé lovingly tells me I will pester any horse until it loves me. And this is not untrue of any trainer gaining trust back that some human has broken. Sometimes the best thing you can do is be there silently; and sometimes the best thing you can do is be there dragging a tarp just because. The back legs were very clearly the biggest issue.

Even looking with intention in their direction or working with my handy stick rewarded me with a terrifyingly well aimed death kick. It was an issue that would last weeks and leave me with a good bruise on my knee a few sessions later. Blankets or things which moved in the wind were another massive issue. Anything which touched his sides or rump resulted in an instant rodeo bronc.

By mid-month we finally walked peacefully through gates, pivoted while you closed them and accepted the saddle blanket on his lower back and withers. As long as it didn't move to touch his hips or flank.

This little horse wasn't the only one making progress in liking his new partner. I fell in love with him more every day. His developing gaits were lovely, and he started to move more freely as he relaxed day by day. The lines in his tense jaw and around his eyes began to smooth.

It was summer and he shed out to a beautiful copper. He looked like new pennies that dusted over him in the sunshine and working him in the evenings with the sunset was a thing normally only found in dreams. At this point in our work, Posey started listening to me. Not obeying or being pushed but listening with a human like intelligence. Some days I admit, he really freaked me out.

To my amazement he had no fear of farm equipment or traffic but what took the most to get him over to this point – feeding time.

I have never seen a horse quite so attached to feed as Posey was. Nights I would take him back to the barn when grain was already in his bin at home he would become superman and physically haul me at the end of the rope into his stall to get to it. He would then panic when I was following him into the stall and start kicking. I knew we had issues one night when I placed him in his stall without food though. He paced and looked at his sides as if he were telling me they hurt. Because of a lesson I learned from Jazzy, who you read about in an earlier chapter of this work, I knew the signs. Ulcers -and why wouldn't he have ulcers? Stressed to the limit from shipping and on a diet with large grain meals spread apart. Posey's saliva glands started anticipating food in the evening which told his stomach to make acid, prepare for digestion. The faster the food got to his stomach the less time raw acid burned him internally. I would rush to my grain too – trainer and rope be damned. I took to grazing him before and after workouts, and we made modifications to his feeding times, and diet as well as treating him for ulcers.

By week three we had started working on letting a lasso be draped over his hips. Pure panic ensued, and I knew it would be a long road to picking up his back feet. We began with the tarp, blankets, squeezing between cones and barrels, jumping barrels, fly spray when the bug season got worse, a surcingle, and at last, a saddle.

A saddle, nothing to be concerned about to most horses even young ones being started when done right, but to Posey it was a cougar on his back. His ulcer pain was yielding and after contracting for another thirty days, on week five we cinched it for the first time. That day Posey proved to me he was fixable. I hate to use that term, because all horses are fixable to a degree if handled with care, and in consideration of their physical and mental limits.

But what he showed me was that he was willing to try yet again with humans. He always gave me every bit of try he had and then sprinkled a little trust on top of it.

That day we got to put a foot in each stirrup. The right side of him was far worse than the left which led me to believe he was a horse that nobody ever led or worked from the right side. This is a common problem I encounter with training horses. I have seen horses which are show trained and just 100% perfect.... unless you need to lead them or get on them from the right side. Because it is common practice to get on and off on the left as well as lead on the left, they have no skill set on the opposite side of their body. When training it is my philosophy to work both sides equally in all things.

By forty-five days, we were riding back and forth across the highway from one barn to the other, and working on liberty work, which helped him to let off some extra nervous energy. Posey had gained the status of my second heart horse after Buck, and I wanted that to last forever. So, when asked one day if I wanted first rights, I made plans to purchase him and informed the owner I would let her know the next evening. She agreed to give me a day to make my decision and make my arrangements.

So, does a horse like Posey get his happy ending?

When I began writing this book, Posey was with his second owner and in training with me following some rotten and quite frankly selfish setbacks from his initial owners when he arrived. I initially wrote the ending to share happily that he was with me, forevermore. But I cannot tell you that is what ultimately happened. In fact, it wrecked me for an entire evening to change the ending to this passage.

You see, Posey was sold out from under me at the very last moment in a deal and shipped north. I called to ask when I should pick him up and was told he just got on a trailer an hour before. It felt a lot like when the bully on the bus offers you a high five, then takes their hand away when you try to complete the action leaving you with nothing but open air and an empty feeling inside. Through a lot of research and time, I tracked him down months later, by stumbling across an ad for the horse he had been sold along with. I remember reaching out and asking if the big sorrel had come in with a little buckskin. At the time the new owner wasn't interested in selling him, so I asked if I could periodically check in just to see how he was doing. If it was the only way I could still be part of his life, I would settle for it.

We checked in here and there for a year or so, and then things went silent. Again I was left with my heart falling through open air. A couple of years passed, then unexpectedly I was contacted by a trainer inquiring on what this buckskin gelding she had acquired knew how to do. She had purchased him from the previous owner who had ghosted me and was working with him. When the trainer began to question where this horse's extensive natural horsemanship knowledge came from, the owner had given her my contact information.

At this time in my life, I was not in a place to purchase him back, but was so relieved to know he was safe. His trainer was kind and I enjoyed beginning to receive riding videos again. Later, I was able to open a place at my farm for Posey, but upon contacting her, I learned she had sold him to an 'older man up North who had a lot of horses in a field', and she had lost the phone number.

I won't mention town names, but the town she provided me with is the location of a well-known horse trader/meat market dealer. This time, my heart fell through open air and slammed into the pavement at the bottom.

Posey's story it seems, may have come full circle back to where he started in a kill pen. I wish with all my heart that I could tell you Posey had a happy ending. But in true life form, we don't always know. The little buckskin is the only horse I have ever told my partner "If Posey shows up - I'm not asking. I'm not talking it over. I will move heaven and Earth to bring him home" Even though he's not a horse guy, he agrees completely. Ladies, get yourself a man like that.

My search ads have gone unanswered for years now, and I have yet to come across him on the great wide internet. But I hope every day that one day Posey can come home to me where he still belongs.

{Chapter 13}

3 Days' Time – Luna

My aunt worked as a nurse in a nursing home for a time. When she met a friend who had horses she was selling, she instantly contacted me. We horse people have all experienced it a million times. People outside of the horse world will send us every little horse-related thing they come across and it's an incredibly sweet thought.

Well, when you rescue horses, people send you every horse ad they see or hear about. And they are right... I want to see them all!

The horses this woman was selling were very nice according to the information she shared with my aunt. One was a show horse and a trail riding horse who were a bonded pair. The woman was in a hurry to get rid of them due to relocating. I waited a few days to contact her but by the time I called, they were already gone.

I had been looking for a show horse to further training on, so I and asked who she had sold them to since she was in a hurry and if they may be interested in reselling the horses to me if I liked them. She informed me she sold them to a horse trader in a small town not so far away. So that was my next step.

I contacted the man and asked about the horses. He had sold one already and the other he hadn't gotten around to riding or advertising. He was thrilled to have someone coming to him before he even put the trouble in to market the other mare.

We set an appointment time and went to look at the lovely bay show mare. Upon arrival I saw quite a few other horses on the property. One of them was in the front pen, saddled, in the blazing July afternoon. Its head had been tied to the back of the saddle in a tight pull, bit and all. The man was chasing it around in circles as it stumbled and threw its mouth open trying to relieve the pressure and escape. How was he supposed to run forward with his head tied around to the back of a saddle? The horse was terrified, and I gave a strongly disapproving glare at the man. He proceeded to tell me that it was real training to 'get em supple'. Looked like torture to me.

I had already been training horses for private clients as well as my rescues for a couple years at that point and saw no need to be so brutal. I asked him what would happen if he made them injure themselves. To my continued horror, his response to me was that he had seen colts break their necks trying to get away and that if they were so stupid, they weren't worth anything anyways. I wanted to cry. I wanted to cry for them all as we walked to the back pen to see at least what I could do for the show mare. I didn't have space for them all. I decided to make an anonymous report later to the local authorities. As for the show mare, he wouldn't let me ride her, but she seemed in great health. He went on and on about how incredibly nice she was and he really liked her because she was short and had a built good. She wasn't built well though. She looked like a hulk situated on toothpick legs, and mini marshmallow hooves. We looked anyways, thinking to save her from any 'training' the man may do. We were informed that if we didn't buy her someone was coming tomorrow to buy her.

I guess he found time to advertise her between my call and our appointment or it was a marketing ploy. Either way, my mother kept looking away from the bay mare, and to a pen further back. We are a pretty tight package deal my mother and I; so when something catches her eye, I know it immediately. What we saw made us both stare in awe.

A huge black mare was in that far away pen, along with a small red roan. The latter of which was beating the daylight out of the mare in the small space. We had to know. Who and what was the black mare. Was she for sale? The object of our desires changed instantly.

As it turns out she was not for sale. Why was this?

Because a meat truck would be there in three days for her.

We were informed with no small amount of sexist condescension that she was dangerous and would kill some little women like us in a heartbeat. I cannot fail to mention that I was taller, younger, and I guarantee physically stronger than the man speaking these words to us at the time. The much smaller red roan he stated, would make something of herself and he planned to start her soon and sell her for a tidy profit. But the black mare had three days' time. My mother, not one to be put off by a condescending tone, and not one to be dissuaded by some little man syndrome, slowly walked back to the 'off limits' pen as we were being told everything about the 'beast'. She crouched by the panel of the pen holding her hand out, palm down for the mare to sniff. She wouldn't come within several feet. The thing we both saw at the same time? Her eyes – they wanted, they needed to trust us. She took a hesitant step, trembled, stepping all over the red lead rope halter combo that had been left on for who knows how long. The rubs on her face indicated it had been a while.

We inquired on her back story, and I was a bit shocked that he actually shared it. According to him, she was a crazy lunatic fence crusher who would kill you given half a chance or less. He wouldn't sell her to anyone because they would end up dead.

Well, that simply wouldn't do. Wehad to have her.

We asked to see the black mare in an open pen, and again for some reason he agreed. I like to think that perhaps some small part of him was redeemable and could see killing her wasn't the only answer, but we will never know. He began the process of shoving her through a network of corral chutes he used for cattle. Swatting and roughly encouraging her forward. Never once did she kick out or try to hurt him as he hurt her. Once she got to the end panel which was a dead end, the fence could be opened into a round pen. She stopped there, chest against the panel which kept her from the relief of open space. Her eyes were wide, her head held high above the panels, and her body shaking. She needed to back up a little to let the last gate slide back. The seller climbed up on top of the panel next to her and grabbed the lead rope. From this elevated position he began pulling it up and back. The mare went right where he told her to. She reared to an impressive height in the stocks and came to land directly on the low hanging electrical lines running above it.

Terror shot through my mother and I. The draped extension cords and electrical wires now supported the top half of the mare, her hind legs still struggling for balance on the dirt below. And what did the seller do? He stood there and looked at her as if it were nothing out of the ordinary until our yelling at him finally prompted him to walk casually to the shed and cut the power from the box. We thanked God she was not electrocuted as she struggled free of the lines, coming down onto the fence panel, and then returned all four feet to the ground.

It was decided. We could not leave her there. It didn't matter if we had to beg, borrow or steal the money, at any price that mare was going in our trailer. A day later, trailer in tow, Buck the buddy horse in place, we picked up our beautiful girl with her new name in place. The mare became known as Luna. Our deal was made with one huge promise – one of the only promises I ever made fully intending to break it - that we would be good little girls and go home and get a male trainer because she would kill us women. We nodded and smiled until we got her into the trailer and headed home to be ours.

Once home, Luna was unloaded from our trailer which was backed directly into the round pen. We had stayed up most of the prior night extending in height with boards and rolls of fencing in case her extreme fence jumping and crushing skills were a fact. She was something to behold. Although underweight and understandably cautious about everything, she had a glistening black coat and naturally wavy tail. Her mane was torn to shreds but it would grow back, and we hoped the bald patches on her face would regrow hair. We didn't know when we got her that she had two beautiful back socks which had been hidden under the mud.

It took almost two weeks to touch her. We let her go at her own pace. It was like being a little kid again and waiting to pet black beauty. Every day I hoped it would be the day. If I just sat there long enough, if I was quiet enough. But I remember the day so well when it finally happened.

I was lying on top of the horse trailer; it was late August now and I was doing what I formally referred to as 'the hick thing'. What's that you ask? Well, tanning on top of my horse trailer while getting some singing and horse bonding time in of course! Ah, multitasking with class.

That day, I stopped singing and turned over to my other side, so I was on my back with the warmth of the sun frying me like a potato chip. I lay there for a second in the quiet listening to the birds and to Luna walking around in the dry round pen, her soft plodding on her giant still untrimmed feet roaming here and there. Until a loud bang sounded and the trailer shook beneath me. A huff of air blew through my hair; warm and inquisitive. I very slowly turned over to my stomach and met Lunas nose in my face. She was standing with one front foot inside the trailer lifting herself up with neck outstretched. Apparently stopping singing had made her think something was incredibly wrong with the strange scrawny horse who stands on its hind feet and brings her food. I thought she would pull away when I turned over, when I gently reached out to touch her nose, or when I started talking to her again. But she never pulled away again.

She had proclaimed it. It was time to get started. As it turned out, she had a solid foundation of groundwork buried under that fear, and it took only a few additional weeks to be in the saddle for what I later was able to confirm was her first ride at age thirteen. We worked with Luna for the next few months before taking her out for her first solo ride. She was spectacular and we were so glad to have her as part of the family. That is not to say we didn't have our bumps. There is no horse journey without some setbacks and adventures.

We had one such adventure together when we used to go riding down the country road. Road signs are always a tossup and often horses' reactions to them vary. Luna feared only one sign of all the available options. A stop ahead sign down the side road of our property. The sign was loose and would sway slightly back and forth on its post as we rode by. One cold fall day it was quite calm outside and we took an afternoon ride. As usual on the way home, Luna started skittering for the far side of the road when we approached the sign, giving it a wide berth.

This particular day, I was determined to get her over the issue. I dismounted, and headed her towards the sign, standing in the ditch in front of it. She stared at it face on, wide eyed as I assured her it was alright to be this close. I didn't move the sign at first but left it still so she could settle. Luna was a quick study in just about everything and soon she was standing with relaxed posture.

I then reached up, and started moving the sign back and forth, as it did when the wind caught it on a breezy day. She was somewhat more alert as the movement began but remained standing with me until –

Plop.

I looked over onto the right shoulder of my coat, and there, in all its glory, was the head of a mouse who I had apparently decapitated staring back at me. Turns out I was rocking someone's home back and forth and when the little guy had popped his head out to see who was at the door – oops. Now I'm not normally what I would consider a girly girl, but you bet I let out a yelp and jumped away from the sign brushing the head with little unseeing eyes from my shoulder. And as for Luna, she lit up, scrambling from the ditch at Mach-one speed and turning back to me as if to say "SEE! I told you it was dangerous!". As I mentioned, Luna was a quick study, and I had just taught her she was right about how terrifying that sign was. I laughed most of the way home and it's still one of my very favorite stories to share. We worked through our fear of the sign on several other outings, and I am glad to say, no additional mice were hurt in the making of this Luna.

When my riding lesson program started several years later, she was an angel who started giving children's lessons. The mare proved herself again and again with both experienced riders and inexperienced riders. She always took care of her person no matter who that was.

In one of the more magical days of my life, I managed to find Lunas first owner who also owned her mother. I got to online chat with this wonderful woman and get some back story on Lunas sire and dam. We also got baby photos! I shared where I had found her and her situation, and we tried to put together the pieces of how she ended up where she did. We were not able to account for some time in her past between our two timelines. But what better reward could there be when you rescue? Her dam's owner and I are still friends to this day.

Our time with Luna came to an end when we fell on some rough times and had to re-home her. We sold her on a buy back contract so she would come straight back to us if ever she needed a place. Hoping we would be able to take on more horses at that time should it ever come to that. Nearly a year later I contacted the owner and asked if she may be interested in selling her back to us because I heard she was headed to college. However, I was given the run around again, and again. I knew once the woman stopped responding to me that Luna was gone, sold to someone, dead, who knew. I would spend the better part of two years watching every social media page that listed horses for sale looking for my Luna.

One night I was hopelessly doing my rounds through a site that listed horses for lease and sale. There on the phone, was a familiar face staring back at me, heart on her forehead and all – Luna by a different name. I remember rubbing my eyes and thinking I was seeing things in my overly tired state. Pulling up old photos, I matched the pattern of the back socks to verify it was her.

A perfect match. She was at a jumping barn with a new owner. She had been to college with this new owner, and she was oh so loved. I have never seen a horse with so many outfits!

Of course I had to contact the new owner. I had spent two years looking, dying to see if she was alright and not back at the meat market path again. My heart was pounding as I sent the message asking if she had perhaps gotten the horse from a girl who seemed a bit, well quite frankly sketchy and whose story hadn't lined up.

"I believe you have my Luna" I typed as I bawled my eyes out huddled in a quilt on my bed. Blessings be, she responded to me.

I told her everything. The current owner finally had the full story on her mare and where she came from. It felt so wonderful to shed some light on her history. I even shared foal photos of Luna I had available. Photos of her first ride, and of us playing around with trick riding and taking her swimming in the creek. What a beautiful feeling it was to share her story. I did inquire whether she would be willing to sell her to me (her ad was for leasing only) and of course the answer was no. Honestly, I think I cried a little harder knowing she was in a place that would never sell her. How could I blame her? Had life not kicked me down, I would never have given this mare up. I was so thrilled Luna had her forever home.

In another kind, and so appreciated offer, we were

allowed to go visit Luna and have closure. We were just a step on her way home to her permanent happy place and we were content with that. Beautiful Luna, who now has a foal all her own, resides happily with her owner and I wish them every single happiness in the future. It's pure joy to know someone loves her just as much as I did.

{Chapter 14}

A Far Away Land – Ollie

Sometimes, the most exotic of things hide in the most ordinary of places. We acquired an additional sort of mystery when we acquired Mina from chapter ten. Among the mares in the pasture that day, darting in and around the round bales was a white pony, who was doing his best impression of a mudslide. Did we need a pony? No. Did we want a pony? Not really. So what did we do? We asked to look at him.

We were informed he sometimes took two or more hours to catch but was ridable. Glutton for punishment as I was, we bought him after only seeing him in the pasture at a good distance.

I believe my exact words were "That looks fun, let's see where that goes."

Delivery day was an exciting one. Storm, my mother's new foal stepped out of the trailer as lovely as we remembered her, followed by Mina, her rather large belly swaying back and forth. Then out of the trailer stepped a pony far smaller than I anticipated him being up close. I had estimated the little guy to be about fourteen one hands, which is fifty-seven inches at the shoulder for my non horse readers. Here, standing in front of me on the freezing

March day in all his glory, was a roughly thirteen hand double coated, mud caked tiny abominable snowman. He had a whopping eleven inches of total saddle space, too small even for my smallest saddles in my lesson program, and he was very extremely gaited.

I have owned a couple of gaited horses in my life. Rocky, my first horse was a Standardbred. We had a mare named Jazz, who was my mother's Saddlebred; and here was the nameless, white gaited pony, who to our astonishment when seen up close, was not a pony at all but an Icelandic horse.

How did a rather rare breed like an Icelandic horse get to the center of the Midwest you ask? I asked the same thing. My investigator hat fits pretty snug once I get on the trail of a horse's past. It rarely blows off my head with setbacks, and stays intact through the good, bad and ugly so I can learn a horse's story.

His future with me was a bit of mystery, I didn't know what I would do with a horse this small, and his past was a bit of a mystery as well. His last point of traceable information was when he was sold at an auction house on the Canadian border.

In doing some research on the breed, I learned a lot of fascinating things. I spoke with a woman representing the breed at a large horse fair in the Midwest as part of that process and learned

Icelandics are the purest breed in the world. Once they were established in their home country, imports of horses were outlawed. This means that at least the horses in Iceland, have been unaltered for over one thousand years. This proud representative of a noble breed, rare, possibly imported, pure and nearly unaltered in modern history – was hanging out in my round pen.

Sometime life is pretty cool.

When we purchased Ollie, we were informed he was ridable. He was friendly in the pens, and I had little trouble catching him after the first week or so of relationship building. Thinking I could possibly use him for some bareback riding days in my lesson program, I set about planning to do a test ride.

Although I was at his recommended weight limit, as covered in another story within this text, balance, intensity, and length of ride matter. Allow me to also insert another fun fact, this breeds recommended carry load is ten percent higher than most horse breeds. It was crucial to put Ollie through his paces before I could safely allow kids to ride him. No one wants an unexpected launch during a lesson. I rode Ollie with an extra thick bareback pad since a saddle was not an option due to space. I'll tell on myself,

it's a good thing I was in better shape then, because my rear just barely fit into the safe zone behind his gaited shoulders but in front of the start of his lumbar spine ...whew, thanks younger me!

As much as I wanted our ride to be smooth, it quickly became clear that something wasn't quite right. While Ollie appeared to know his cues and was gaiting beautifully, it wasn't long before he would unexpectedly erupt into crow hops, tossing his head and skittering sideways until I had no choice but to - well, gracefully step off. There was no real aggression behind his behavior, and no signs of fear. In fact, his reactions didn't resemble any of the typical signs of poor training or a mischievous streak. What caught my attention, however, was his eyes. When we rode, they became expressions of pain—tight, worried, and distant. Concerned, we contacted our vet to investigate further. The diagnosis came back: Ollie had kissing spines, a condition where the vertebrae in a horse's back touch, causing significant discomfort and pain. This

often is aggravated by the downward pressure of a rider on the back. Saddened, I reached out to his previous owner to see if they'd ever noticed similar behavior, such as the bucking or hopping. Their response was disheartening.

Apparently, the husband, who was far oversized for a small horse had ridden Ollie frequently after a sometimes hours long battle to catch him; and while they acknowledged his fussing, they brushed it off with the comment, "He was too small to buck him off."

It's with a deep sigh and the utmost respect for sensitivity that I want to clarify my position. I don't have any issue with people's personal body weight or shape. Never have, never will. But I do have an issue when someone rides a horse that isn't built or conditioned to carry them. It's not fair to the animal;

and Ollie's case is a painful reminder of the consequences. With a sore back exacerbated by inappropriate weight, it's no wonder he tried to escape whenever he was approached by a human.

It's heartbreaking to think that he'd been labeled difficult or evasive without anyone ever checking for underlying pain. It's such a shame that no one considered the reason behind his behavior sooner. If they had, perhaps he could have been spared some of the suffering he endured. All horses deserve that consideration.

After riding lessons were no longer an option for Ollie, we began to look towards things that could enrich his days but respect his physical limits. He has learned quite a few tricks and spent a good number of years playing unicorn in photoshoots for some of my mother's clients on special theme days. With ten pounds of personality in a five-pound bag, he's always a hit. Somehow there was room left for an extra pound of mischief as well.

Being a mythical unicorn is hard work. You must be up early, in the spa, taking a bath and eating cookies. He has many a four AM morning stood – sometimes less than patiently – while his mane and tail are turned into a rainbow of colors for that day's photoshoots. On occasion he's added something a little extra to the mix.

On the day in question, I bathed Ollie in yet another 4 am bath and let him dry. Then, tied at the trailer had begun working on coloring his tail. Ollie had a habit of moving his rear back and forth while I worked, saying no thanks to brushing, and the long, long process of coloring.

On this day, I was delighted with his patience. He had not moved once. I settled in with my headphones in to get his tail completed while he was being so patient. Then I realized something most mothers will relate to.

It was quiet. Too quiet.

I walked to his head to see that he was ok. It was not his habit to fall asleep during this part of the day. I arrived at the front to watch as Ollie plucked one of the colored chalk sticks (yes, nontoxic) I had left on the wheel well of the trailer, out of its holder like a diva plucking chocolate from a box. He munched happily, adding this new yellow slobber to the array of blue, purple, and green already streaming from his mouth and down his pure white neck and chest. Guess he felt there needed to be a little more magic color for that day's sessions.

Our little love never lost his mischievous spirit as the years caught up to him. He had earned his retirement and spent his days in our pasture playing cool uncle to our younger horses and inspiring future children's books I would like to write with his quirky personality. Ollie was never asked to carry a rider or saddle again. He lived a beautiful life, despite his medical issues, despite setbacks and life re-routing changes. From Canada, possibly even Iceland, to the Midwest, and our humble pasture, he inspired awe and joy in whoever crossed his path and spread brightness throughout the world; Ollie was a beautiful reminder that even through challenges, we too can choose to shine.

{Chapter 15}

The Christmas Horse – Dancer

I considered a lot of horses for the final chapter of this book. I considered Posey with his long journey, Luna with her happy ending, or Buck or Zee as definitively the most influential horses of my life. But a few things made this last story perfect for its position.

One, I'll give you a spoiler. It has a happy ending; and two, this book was originally scheduled to come out just prior to the holiday season and this is one of my favorite Christmas time memories of all. Despite moving the release date, I could not bring myself to move Dancer's tale from the ending. The gentle joy of the holidays is something we could use more of year-round. So, regardless of whether the sun is blazing, or the snow is falling while you take in these words, thank you from the bottom of my heart for reading the stories of these animals who meant so much, I hope you enjoy, The Christmas Horse.

"You wanna buy a couple Arabians?" my farrier asked from his bent position while trimming Bucks feet. He knew I bought, trained, and sold the occasional rehab or project horse.

"Nope" I remember answering bluntly "I don't need any more horses."

"I got a couple out at the ranch that we're looking to rehome" he continued as if I hadn't denied my needing to expand the collection. I told him I would be glad to hear about them and let any horse friends I knew looking for a new partner in on the details. This, friends, is where I went wrong. There is a saying that states when you're being mugged you 'never go to the second location,' well with horses and a habit, you 'never ask for the additional details' it's all a self inflicted trap. I walked up to, looked at, smiled, and walked straight into that trap, just as he knew I would. My farrier is an awesome dude, and I am so grateful he threw out the bait.

We arrived at the ranch to meet the two potential horses. One, a middle-aged bay show gelding and the other, an older flea-bitten grey trail gelding. The bay was not built in a way that promised long term soundness. It is with some guilt that I describe him as looking like he had been made on one of those toys children play with where you can mix and match rubbing plates, then draw over them to create whatever combination of animals you choose. Nothing on him quite matched which concerned me for his long-term working ability. In fact, he was lame the day we went to see them and therefore it was immediately not my choice. The grey was incredibly well put together in his basic bone structure despite lacking fat and muscle over those bones. He reminded me of a white reindeer with his large expressive eyes, his mile long legs, and delicate build. All that was missing was the silver antlers.

This special guy needed a new home because he had quite a lot of trouble maintaining weight within a herd. He wasn't going to make effort to push his way up by the round bale and had some anxiety on top of that with being bullied by the other horses. This happens quite commonly in herds. I mean, if every time I went to take a bite of a cheeseburger, someone bullied me away from it, I would lose a few pounds too. Maybe I need to try that... I digress.

Grey as they called him, was not a rescue to be clear. He was a private purchase who was taken care of and simply needed a slightly altered lifestyle to thrive. My mother was fairly set against more horses coming home.

We rented a facility together and as horses always are, it was a lot of work. In addition, her heart ached still for those who were rehomed all those years ago including Rocket from chapter one. How could she welcome another horse when those she loved were out there who knows where? We talked over the horses, and I asked to ride the grey one anyway. It's not something I would do on a thin horse often, but I needed to verify he wasn't a wild child before agreeing to take him on. He love nipped us as we groomed him and once aboard, he (mostly) carried me well around the arena. Except the corners. Most horse owners know shadow beasts live in the corners that only horses can see. He would go along fine, then turn his head like a bird looking through the eye on the side of its face and skitter and crow hop away from the corner monsters, only to regain a nice gait along the straights. But what I felt while on his back was complete and utter peace.

Some horses have loud energy, just like some people. And some have no energy at all, also like some people. But once in a while you meet 'the one' so to speak.

A partner who whispers energy so quietly you lean in closer to listen. That folks, is a special kind of magic. I dismounted, and untacked him after, considering carefully. He had a short show record, stilts for legs, and the kindest of hearts. He was perfect for my mother.

She refused me of course. She was experienced with horses but how could this horse, one of her least favorite colors, older, possessing hardly any teeth, and needing weight; who crow hopped at corners, and could never replace her lost horses be the horse for her?

It was my turn to return the kindness and intuition she had taught me all those years ago when she found Zee for me. I handed her the lead rope.

"Take him for a walk to the other side of the paddock, and if you don't feel it, I won't argue."

She came back to the barn door, leggy Arabian in tow, and with a teary smile. She felt his energy just as I did in all its perfection.

Winston Churchill once said, "There is something about the outside of a horse that is good for the inside of a man" Truer words never spoken. There was something undefinable about Dancer's very being, that was good for my mother's heart and soul.

By the time we got a delivery schedule arranged, and the day arrived, it was early December. Dancer, as he was now named, settled into his stall at our facility like a king to his throne. He adored having his own feed, his own buckets, and his own space. He was a curious horse with stunning globe eyes, and more expression than you could pack into an artist's convention. His muzzle so soft it felt like a rose petal, and his talkative nicker began to fill the barn each morning in greeting.

We fell more in love every day.

Every year around Christmas, the local historical site mansions in our area put on a collection of tours in which the public can travel around on buses and visit the three to four sites. Over the years we have been lucky enough to participate at a couple of the tours in historical dress, or as part of the experience in another way. One such mansion has an original stable. The year we purchased Dancer, there was a last-minute cancellation and the man who normally filled the spot of 'Christmas horse' with his gelding needed a fill in. We were mid stall cleaning process, smelling to all the world like manure and barn when he walked through the door.

"You have any horse you could take as a Christmas horse for the manor?"

"I don't know, we have owned him for like a week, he seems chill, let's do it. But -" I glanced at the mudball masquerading as my mother's horse and then down at myself

"you're going to have to give me like an hour to bathe both him and me." So it was that Dancer loaded into an oversized draft trailer, and we traveled to the venue in hopes he would cooperate for the event.

We learned a lot of things about partnership with him that day. One, thank goodness he was comfortable with traffic because our ride dropped us in a local church parking lot across a busy road from the mansion and left us immediately. Two, that he would walk just about anywhere, but vintage cobblestones were a totally new feel to his feet and sound to his ears. His hoofbeats echoed around the empty courtyard walls, harkening back to a time when horses were a pride of the manor. Not at all cognizant of the magical moment we were having stepping back in time; Dancer began turning his head sideways pointing an eye and ear at the ground as if it would eat him as he begrudgingly took tiptoe step after step for his crazy new humans who were asking crazy new things.

Once in the courtyard of the historic site, we were to meet the event coordinator and then put him in the stable and hang tight until the event started.

However, there was no coordinator to be found.

Here we were, standing in the mansion courtyard with a light grey nearly white Arabian horse as the snow began. And while he would likely not have been historically accurate to the original scene (Based on my research, for the status of the family and the time it would have most likely been a Saddlebred.) I couldn't help wishing I had a camera easily accessible at the time. We set about locating a person who could let us into the locked stable door. After knocking on several doors at intervals around the courtyard and praying Dancer would handle it well when one finally opened like a jack in the box to reveal a person; we were kindly greeted by the coordinator who was expecting a call from the trailer driver when we arrived. She gladly opened the doors and gave us the rundown of the evening for the event.

Once inside the barn, we realized another time period specific feature of the stable. While modern stalls are often equipped with thick rubber mats to stop slipping, these historic beauties at the estate were made from extremely slick, high gloss, green vintage tiles. These are original to the stables, and nearly one hundred years old. I don't know if I have ever been so glad to have a horse who treads so daintily. We spread some pine bedding to help

Dancer's hooves with the slippery surface and awaited the holiday crowds.

Dancer, the elegant, kind, gentle, doe eyed love is – well, a complete pig in any dirt he can get around, and a ham with any people he can get around. He delightedly spent his entire evening greeting people as they walked into the stable from the mansion having nearly finished their tour. He wore a massive red Christmas bow around his neck with glowing pride, and whenever someone would pet him and turn to leave the stable, he was convinced it was his duty to travel with them into the snow outside the doors. He would only 'forget' that mission upon another group entering the aisle to pamper him with pets and smiles. I like to think the past owner of the stable who was from my research a true horse lover, was smiling down at us and how special it was to have another soft nosed, winter fluffy, equine in her stables.

As our evening drew to a close, we packed up, cleaned up, and made our way out into the now dark courtyard. We needed to cross the street again to make our way back to the trailer which was waiting in the church lot for us to arrive. Many things are different to a horse in the dark. Sometimes something that seemed perfectly safe in the light is no longer considered a viable option in the dark. Sometimes, the place we passed on the way in looks nothing like the place we pass on the way out. The church had a special event happening as well. A live nativity, complete with real moving humans, sheep, a donkey, and... a camel. A very loud, opinionated camel. As it turns out, Dancer was not a fan of the "humpback horse" who made funny noises. At the sight of it, he began a prance that would have made any dressage rider proud.

Eventually, he settled—though he kept one eye out for that "lumpy llama" the whole way around the massive buildings parking lot. Once we reached the back lot, we were greeted with blindingly bright lights from inside the oversized draft horse stock trailer. It looked like a spaceship had landed. I am sure with its lights, and huge ramp looking like a portal to somewhere far away, that the trailer seemed a lot like being led into the light for Dancer. After blinking away the dots in his squinting vision, he loaded into the massive trailer. I remember even his tall height looked miniature in the space meant for draft horses.But as usual, he let us lead him into the unknown. What a horse.

Our Dancer is still with us today. He's retired from being my mother's riding horse after years spent enjoying trips up and down the country roads near our home, a couple of 'comeback' horse shows where I was honored to be aboard his back. He has taught many of my special needs students' confidence, communication, strength, and the love of horses while in his care.

He's a forever keeper, with a best friend in our pasture, and a heart full of quiet he gently shares with all who meet him. His story, much like the stories of so many horses who come into our lives, is one of trust, love, and the quiet miracles that unfold when we open our hearts to these gentle souls. And although his gallop has slowed, the spirit in his eyes reminds us every day that the journey we walk with horses is one we carry forever in our hearts.

Afterword

As I bring A Road of Rescued Hearts: Rescue Horse Stories of Faith, Trust, and Miracles to a close, I find myself reflecting on the personal journey that has unfolded alongside the stories of these incredible horses. Many of the horses you've read about were not just names in a book, they were part of my life, my world, and my heart. Each one challenged me in ways I never expected, and each one rewarded me with lessons I'll never forget.

Rescue and rehabilitation work has always been deeply personal to me. It's not just about giving a horse a second chance; it's about giving them a piece of my heart, trusting in the process, and walking with them through their fears, uncertainties, and pain. There were moments of frustration, doubt, and exhaustion, but every step of the journey was worth it when I saw the light return to their eyes, when I felt their trust begin to bloom or when I saw their bodies beginning to heal.

These horses weren't just projects or stories; they were companions, friends, and teachers. They taught me about patience when I thought I had none left, about resilience in the face of setbacks, and about unconditional love, something I have found repeatedly when I walked into a dusty barn or a muddy pasture and saw a scared, broken horse slowly start to believe in me.

Together, we learned that trust doesn't happen overnight, and healing is a journey we must take one step at a time.

The bond I've built with each of these horses is something words can barely describe. It's a connection that runs deep, a silent understanding that reminds me why I do this work in the first place. They've shown me that no life is too far gone to be saved, that miracles happen when we have the faith to keep going, even when the road gets tough.

I hope that as you've read their stories, you've been able to glimpse into the lives of these horses and understand how transformative rescue, rehabilitation, and partnership can be—not just for the animals, but for those who are willing to give their hearts to the process.

Thank you for walking this road with me, and for seeing the beauty and possibility in each of these rescued hearts. It's been my honor to share this journey with you, and I hope it inspires you to embrace your own path of love, compassion, and second chances.

With heartfelt gratitude,

Elowyn Hale

Acknowledgements

This book and the stories within would not have been possible without the help of my amazing Mother Catherine, who must have read every line a thousand times during the writing process. Thanks also to my incredibly supportive partner David who believes in me even on the days I don't believe in myself.

Further thanks to my amazing group of beta readers, and my editor Justin Rajkowski for helping me make these stories to be very best they can be.

Glossary

Arabian (horse breed): An ancient breed of horse valued for its speed, stamina, beauty, and gentleness. Originating from the Arabian Peninsula.

Bay (horse color): A bay horse will have a dark brownish body color as well as a black muzzle and legs.

Botfly: A parasitic fly which infects a horse's intestines with eggs causing potential digestive issues.

Buckskin (horse color): A shade resembling tanned hide or butterscotch.

Conformation: It refers to the horse's overall physicality. A horse with good conformation will have proper body proportions for its breed and age. Horses with bad conformations have damaged bone structures.

Coronet: The layer of skin that the hoof grows from.

Crow Hop: When a horse gives a small buck.

Downhill build: Having a build in which the shoulders sit lower than the level of the pelvis.

Farrier: A farrier specializes in working with a horse's hooves. Farriers trim a horse's feet and apply horseshoes.

Filly: Young female horse, generally younger than five years.

Foal: Term used for a male or female horse under one year old.

Gaited: A horse that can perform one or more gaits other than walk, trot, canter and gallop.

Gelding: A neutered male horse.

Green broke: A green broke horse has just begun its training and is not very good with riders. The term usually references horses that have been ridden under the saddle at least a few times.

Hand: We use hands to measure the height of horses. One hand is 4 inches long in this case.

Lame: A lame horse can't walk or run properly anymore because it experiences constant pain in one of its legs.

Lunging: A training method wherein a human uses a long line and encourages structured movement in training.

Mare: A female horse.

Morab: A cross of Arabian and Morgan horse breeds.

Muzzle: A horse's nose.

Palomino (horse color): Genetic color in horses, consisting of a gold coat and white mane and tail.

Posting: Also known as a rising trot. The act of the rider rising from the saddle in time with the horse's gait.

Quarter Horse: A compact, muscular horse whose name is derived from the breeds' ability to outrun other horse breeds in a quarter mile or less race.

Saddlebred: A gaited breed originating in the U.S.

Sorrel (horse color): A coat color of copper-red.

Standardbred: A breed developed in North America most associated with harness racing.

Sulky: Type of cart used in Standardbred horse racing.

Tobiano (coat pattern): Pinto marking with patches of white that stretch from the back of the horse to its sides.

About the Author

Elowyn Hale is a passionate storyteller and equine enthusiast. Raised in the Midwest, she discovered her deep connection with horses early on, spending countless hours involved in equestrian sports, care, and rescue.

Her writing journey began with a desire to share the often overlooked stories of special horses and the people who find healing through their bond with these majestic animals.

Elowyn's love for storytelling extends into the realms of fiction, where she explores themes of courage, redemption, and the enduring human (and sometimes inhuman) spirit.

When not writing, she enjoys painting, spending time with her horses, and singing.

To learn more, explore her latest, and upcoming works, or join her growing community of readers follow her @ElowynHaleAuthor on social media.